Bartending Basics
A Complete Beginner's Guide
by
Thomas Morrell

Copyright Notice

Trademark Disclaimer

Copyright Acknowledgement

Legal Disclaimer

What is the difference between God and a bartender?

Answer: God does not think he is a bartender.

Table Of Content

Preface.. Pg. 7

<u>Chapter 1</u> Beer... Pg. 9

<u>Chapter 2</u> Wine... Pg. 27

<u>Chapter 3</u> Distilled Spirits.. Pg. 45

<u>Chapter 4</u> Bartending Equipment & Terms...................... Pg. 63

<u>Chapter 5</u> Mixing Cocktails... Pg. 75

<u>Chapter 6</u> Customer Service.. Pg. 101

<u>Chapter 7</u> Working In The Bar... Pg. 113

<u>Chapter 8</u> Responsible Bartending................................... Pg. 139

<u>Chapter 9</u> Finding A Job.. Pg. 163

<u>Afterword</u>.. Pg. 179

<u>Appendix</u> Basic Drink Recipes... Pg. 181

<u>Preface</u>

I work in the hospitality industry and have since I was thirteen years old. It is what I do and it is what I know. Specifically, I work in restaurants. I have done everything there is to do in a restaurant. I have been a busboy, dishwasher, host, cook, waiter, manager and lastly a bartender. This last occupation is what this book is about. Far and away, this is my favorite activity in a restaurant. When you are behind the bar, you are in control of it all. Men accord you respect and the ladies look on with awe. It is a liberating and empowering experience that needs to be lived to be understood.

A bartending career can also offer you many advantages. First of all, there is the money. Bartenders make lots of money in tips and take cash home every night. There is no need to wait for a paycheck. Bartending also offers lots of flexibility. I worked as a bartender the entire time I was in college. I know plenty of bartenders who take care of their children during the day while their spouse is at work. At night, they work and their spouse cares for the children. Bartending is also the type of job you can go anywhere in the world to do, any town in this country has a bar and needs someone to pour the drinks. I know bartenders that have lived on Caribbean islands and worked as bartenders on cruise ships as well. Your options are wide and many with a bartending career.

Many people have approached me during the years (some have even rudely called during a Saturday night rush to ask) how one becomes a bartender. They want to be back there. This book is the answer to all those questions and is about how I became a bartender and how you can too. Inside I will tell you how you can do the same things I have done and go where I have gone.

When I originally started working as a server, I was exposed to a number of bartenders who had attended a bartending school. I did not attend one of these and pulled myself up on my own, learning as I went. These schools can be very expensive and I thought that a self study book with a similar curriculum and tests would be appreciated by all those people out there who longed to do what I do.

This book is the product of that idea. You will find that the layout contained in these covers is that of a textbook. You will be presented with a body of text that discusses one aspect of being a successful bartender. You will need to read through this text and digest the information it contains. Along with facts, techniques and concepts, you will also find many examples thrown in as well. These are used to further illustrate a point or philosophy that I have regarding a particular subject. At the end of each chapter you will find a series of review questions or a homework assignment. I have found that these tools often help to reinforce what a person has just read and further plant the ideas contained in the chapter.

Now, the subtitle of this book is "A Complete Beginner's Guide". Pay attention to that for a second. Contained in this book are only the basic tools, techniques and concepts that are needed to become a bartender. Reading and studying this book does not guarantee any success in this career path. You will need to put forth a great deal of effort, patience, and hard work if you are to be successful. You need to have a good mindset and a friendly personality if you wish to rise to the top. You need to memorize your recipes and thoroughly understand the ideas presented here. However, with hard work and discipline, and the ideas and concepts in this book, there is no reason that you cannot one day stand confidently behind the bar.

-Thomas Morrell

Chapter 1
Beer

When beer was discovered by humans is a fact that will probably never be known. We do know that beer was a staple food of the Ancient Mesopotamians and Egyptians and made up a large percentage of their diet. The point is that beer has been around for thousands of years and humans love it. Beer consumption in the world continues to rise each year as countries like China (the world's largest beer consumer) continue to develop and refine their taste for the beverage.

Beer is one of the many things you will be pouring into glasses as a bartender so you will need to be familiar with it. It used to be the case that a bar would only carry several mass produced pilsner style beers. This has changed. American beer drinkers have developed many wide and varying tastes for different beer styles from across the globe. Exotic imported English brown ales share tapboards with German lagers, Irish stouts and Mexican or Chinese pilsners. I know bars that proudly offer over one hundred beers on draft alone with even more in the bottle.

Most of the readers of this book will be familiar with beer through having consumed it. However, you should know more than that as a bartender. You will need to understand the basic process of making beer. You will also need to know the difference between and be able to differentiate various beers. You need to know how to pour a beer for maximum enjoyment. You will need to know how to taste beer. Lastly, you need to be able to talk beer and communicate ideas such as flavors to your guests. We will discuss all of these ideas and techniques in this chapter of the book.

The Process Of Making Beer

Making beer is a fairly simple process that can take years to master. In a nutshell, you cook water, a type of grain (this is usually a malted barley and maybe wheat) and hops to make a sugary liquid call wort. This liquid is then placed in a vessel known as a fermenter where it is cooled and a small amount of bacteria called yeast is introduced to the mix and the batch is allowed sit.

Yeast is a remarkable type of bacteria that is extremely valuable to humans. This primitive single celled type of bacteria survives by "eating" sugar. The sugar undergoes a chemical process whereby the sugar molecule is converted to alcohol, carbon dioxide and energy for the yeast cell. This energy is used by the yeast to reproduce and make other yeast cells to eat more sugar, make more alcohol, sugar and energy and to reproduce again. This process is repeated millions and millions of times in a fermenter until all of the sugar has been "eaten". Yeast is actually responsible for every type of alcoholic beverage and naturally occurs on many types of fruits and grains as well as in the air.

Once the yeast has finished its work the beer may go through further processing including filtering, bottling and or kegging. Many types of beers are not filtered. Unfiltered beers are often produced by "microbrews", craft brewers or home brewers because of the ease of production and great flavor that is present without filtering. The yeast left in the beer is actually very high in vitamins and adds to the nutritional value of the beer.

Ingredients In Beer

Barley

The main ingredient in beer is a grain of some form. This can be many different types of grain, but it is by far most often barley. The barley that is processed into beer is known as malted barley. This means that the grain was soaked in water and allowed to germinate slightly. This causes the sugar content of the grain to rise dramatically. Malted barley makes a stronger alcoholic beverage than would be possible without the malting process.

The brewing process always begins with a grains like these shown above. Traditional beers use barley and wheat although beer can be made from other grains such as millet and rice.

Once the grain has begun to germinate it is placed in a kiln and dried. By controlling the heat of the kiln, how quickly it heats up, and how long the grain is left in the kiln, different types of malts can be created. Popular types of malt include pale malt, crystal malt, chocolate malt and even black malt (almost burned). The different types of malts all offer different flavor characteristics and can be blended by brewers to create complex and varying beers with a wide range of tastes.

Before the grain is cooked in a kettle to make the wort, it is ground into finer particles. This allows more of the sugar to be extracted by the water during the cooking process.

Hops

Hops are the other main ingredient in beer (other than water of course). The hop plant is a tall creeping vine that grows rapidly each season. The hops that are used by brewers are actually the female flowers of the plant. The flowers are rich in complex plant oils that give the tart crispness to beer as well as contributing a great deal of the potency to the aroma at the head of the beer. These sensations often balance the sweetness in beer and help to create a more complex and balanced taste sensation.

The hop plant a winding vine. The flowers are the actual ingredients used in the brewing process. The help preserve the beer and add an enjoyable bitterness. Photo courtesy of Hop Growers of America (www.usahops.org) .

Hops do more than just flavor beers to which they are added. They also help preserve the beer. This is thought to be one of the main reasons that adding hops to beers became popular.

Beer Vocabulary

Since you will be serving beer in you bar, you will need to know how to talk about beer to your guests. Also, a basic vocabulary for discussing beer will be very helpful in understanding the discussion of beer styles that follow.

Buzzwords are the name of the game when it comes to discussing flavors. These words help the guests to understand the taste sensation they can expect before they commit to ordering a particular beer. What follows is a short list of beer buzzwords and a more detailed explanation of what they mean. You should consider these words to be an indispensable part of your beer education and you should commit them to memory. The first time a guest asks you to describe a beer, you will be happy you did.

Malty - Malty is a buzzword that is used to describe the sweetness in a beer. This is a good word to use when you want to emphasize that the sweet flavor in the beer is dominant over the bitterness added by the hops.

Hoppy – Hoppy is just the opposite of malty. This word is best used when you want to emphasize that the bitterness imparted by the hops is the dominant flavor.

Dry - Dry is a word that is used to convey a lack of sweetness. This quality comes about from most of the sugars in the beer having been turned into alcohol during the fermentation process.

Sweet – Use this word to describe beers where a good portion of the sugar remains after fermentation. This word is especially useful with beers that are fruit infused.

Undertone – A subtle flavor present in the beer. This often appears as an aftertaste and is secondary to the dominant flavor.

Light – Use this word to describe beer that does not have a syrupy physical consistency, especially beers that are refreshing. Pale ales often fall into this category.

Crisp – This is a good word to describe beers that have a bitter taste from hops, but are light in body. This is a good word to describe an IPA.

Finish – This word describes the taste sensation after the beer has been swallowed. This word is similar in use to "aftertaste".

Types Of Beers

While not technically one of the ingredients in beer, yeast is incredibly important to the finished product that is beer. There are many different types of yeast that are used in modern brewing. Many brewers jealously guard their yeasts. Each of these types of yeast, called strains, offers different characteristics. There are two main strain types. These are top fermenting yeasts and bottom fermenting yeasts. Top fermenting yeasts concentrate their activities in the top part of the fermenter, while bottom fermenting yeasts become more concentrated at the bottom.

The two main types of beers, are a product of this fact. The first of these types, the ales, are created using top fermenting yeast. The other type of beer, the lagers, are created using bottom fermenting yeasts. Ales are often lighter, fruity flavored beers, while lagers generally offer more in the way or a crispness.

Lagers

Lagers are an extremely popular set of beers that any bar will carry. The most popular beer brands in the world are lager style beers; however, you will generally only see a few distinct lager styles represented in your bar.

Pilsners

This lager style beer is a light, hoppy, golden colored brew that was originally brewed in Bohemia in the 19th century. Since then it has been widely imitated. Many of the world's most popular beers are pilsner style beers. As a result of this, pilsner style beers are the most popular and widely sold beer in the modern beer market. Pilsner style beers are generally a little low in terms of their alcohol content. You will frequently see these beers containing around 5% alcohol by volume.

Bock

Bock is a popular, darker ale style that is generally associated with Germany, Austria and the Netherlands. The color of this beer is generally a strong amber tone. This beer is specially brewed in Germany for festivals in the colder months and would likewise be a good suggestion for your guests during winter. Bocks generally have a higher alcohol content of around 6.5%. These beers are often treated after brewing by freezing. Some of the water in the beer freezes and can be removed making a stronger beer. Beers that have gone through this process are called eisbock.

Abbey Style Beers

Abbey style beers are produced exclusively in Belgium. These light beers are often reddish-brown in color with a distinctively fruity flavor and aroma. This beer style was started by monks in Belgium but is now carried on by commercial companies operating under license from the abbeys, for the most part.

Ales

Most bars will carry a wide selection of ales. This beer class is easy to brew and is subject to a great deal of experimentation and innovation from smaller regional breweries around the country. Beer styles like chocolate stouts, cream ales, and cherry infused ales have become common. As a result of this there has been an explosion of beer connoisseurs who are specific in their tastes but enjoy finding and trying something new as well. A good bartender will be their guide.

Pale Ale

Pale ale is the quintessential English beer. This style is generally amber in color and light in body. Additionally, this style is known for a crisp hoppy flavor in the finish. This style is incredibly popular with microbreweries and will be part of any small brewery's offerings.

IPA

The anacronym that makes up this beer's name stands for India Pale Ale. During their colonization of India and other parts of the world, British soldiers and citizens still wanted to have a classic English pale ale. It had long been known that hops helped preserve a beer. So, to overcome the long time and distance during sea travel to their colonies, British brewers began adding extra high levels of hops to their beers. This style generally has an alcohol content of around 6% and is widely produced by specialty ale brewers. This beer will be very popular with guests that like a very crisp and hoppy taste to their beer.

Bitter

Bitter is by far the most popular draft beer in England. This is actually a more mild form of the traditional pale ale style. Contrary to what its name might imply bitter is generally lower in hops than pale ales or IPAs and often has a sweeter flavor than these other English beers. This beer style is usually a reddish, amber color with an alcohol content of around 3-5%.

An increasingly popular variant of this beer, in the United States, is ESB. This anacronym stands for Extra Special Bitter. This beer is generally also a reddish, amber color. The special distinction between this beer and the basic bitter style is that this brew frequently has a much higher alcohol content.

Brown

Brown ale is another traditional English beer. This beer style can range in color from medium amber to dark brown or almost black. The predominant flavor characteristic of brown ale is a sweet maltiness. There is usually little hop flavor present in a brown ale. Brown ales are less common from domestic breweries, but are growing in popularity. However, there are a number of bottled English brown ale brands that are popular among beer drinkers and are widely available.

Porter

Porter is a dark brown to black ale that was originally brewed in London in the early 18th century. It has been suggested that the porter style developed from the habit of pub owners pouring several different brews into a single pint. The origins of the name "porter" are somewhat murky; however, the name may have come from the beer being popular with early railroad porters and other hard working blue collar laborers in London. Porter is a very commonly brewed ale style. This heavy brew is very popular in the winter months. The flavor of porter is generally mild and malty with much less emphasis on the hops.

Stout

Stout is another very dark ale that is made by the addition of a dark malted barley to the brewing process. Also, this type of beer is heavily hopped giving the beer a dry quality. Another characteristic of stout is a thick creamy consistency.

Irish stout is far and away the most popular form of stout. You will almost definitely pour one of these in any bar you will work in. This popularity is due to the advertising efforts of a certain Irish stout brewers. However, there are many other styles of stouts that you may encounter. These include oatmeal stout, Russian Imperial stout (actually another English style stout) and chocolate stout. These specialty stouts are often produced by microbreweries that cater to a niche market.

Wheat Beers

Wheat ale is a type of ale that is made from a grain mix of both malted barley and wheat. This mix imparts a softer flavor to the beer and often results in a sweeter beer.

Mixes of this kind can be brewed into either a lager or an ale. Southern Germany is well known for lager style wheat beers, while the German style Hefeweizen is a well known wheat ale. In addition to these two styles, many German breweries will also produce a Dunkelweizen. This style of wheat ale is a dark wheat that is common in any German pub.

Hefeweizen style beers are incredibly popular in America today, especially during the Summer months. This type of wheat ale is most often served with a lemon. This is a tradition that would have helped address the problem of bacteria and spoilage in the beer prior to the development of refrigeration. Today, it is used as a flavor additive only.

Non-Alcoholic Beers

Non-alcoholic beer is a misleading term. Non-alcoholic beers usually contain alcohol; however, the amount that these beers contain is generally lower than the level that requires government regulation. In the United States, a beer can legally be called non-alcoholic if it contains .5% alcohol or less.

Non-alcoholic beers, often called "near beer" or "NA beer", were very popular during Prohibition and many large breweries survived that period through the sale of non-alcoholic beers. Today, many well known brands or non-alcoholic beer are produced by all the major breweries. These beers are generally a light pilsner style beer or a mild, light amber.

Beer Mixes

You will frequently encounter requests for beer mixes. These are either two types of beer mixed together or beer served with a mixer. There are five major beer mixes that will pop up from time to time in any bar, although only occasionally.

Black & Tan – A "Black & Tan" is a traditional mix of Bass™ Pale Ale and Guinness™ Dry Irish Stout. Fill the glass half way with Bass™ and then, float the Guinness on top of the ale. This can be tricky and will take a little practice.

Snakebite – A Snakebite is a half and half mix of hard cider and lager beer.

Black Adder – A Black Adder is a half and half mix of hard cider with Guinness™ floated on top.

Shandy – A Shandy is a mix of lager beer and lemon & lime soda. Generally the mix is half and half. In addition to lemon & lime soda, lemonade, ginger ale, and soda water can be used.

Red Beer – Red beer is a mix of lager beer and tomato juice. The tomato juice can be served in the mix at 25%, 50% or can be served on the side in another glass for the guest to add at will.

Beer In The Bar

In the bar where you will be working, beer will come in three possible packaged forms. These are bottles, cans, and kegs.

Bottled beer will generally come in a 12 ounce or 22 ounce brown, green or clear glass bottle. These are most often capped in the usual way and are opened with a bottle opener. Some specialty and European bottled beers will be sealed with a champagne cork style closure. These bottles are opened by unwinding and removing the wire retaining frame and pulling the cork by hand. Always point these corks away from anyone before opening them. The corks on these bottles can fly out and may cause injury!

Bottled beers do not require refrigeration and are often stored at room temperature. Many bars will have a premium on refrigerated space and will only keep a small percentage of their bottled beer supply cold to be served to guests immediately.

Canned beer is far less common in most bars, but it is possible that it will be served in the bar you ultimately work in. Canned beers will be in 12 ounce or 16 ounce cans. Opening a beer can is simple. Just pop the top. There is nothing special to it.

Canned beer like bottled beer does also not require refrigeration. These, if your bar carries them, will most likely also be stored at room temperature with the bottled beer and only a small portion will be kept cold for immediate service.

The overwhelming majority of the beer you will serve will be in kegs. Kegs are metallic barrels that hold beer. In the United States, the standard keg size is 15.5 gallons. Beer is forced out of the kegs by the use of a pressurized gas.

Connecting a keg to the tap system is called "tapping a keg". This requires connecting a coupler to the keg and turning on the gas.

Carbon dioxide is the standard gas that is used to pour beer. This gas makes up a large percentage of the air you are breathing while you read this. It is colorless, odorless and does not impart any flavor to the beer and is responsible for the characteristic bubbles in beer.

In addition to carbon dioxide, beer can also be poured using nitrogen. This is another gas that is present in air. In fact, nitrogen gas makes up almost 60% of the Earth's atmosphere. Nitrogen is also a colorless odorless gas that does not add any flavor to the beer. However, nitrogen pours beer somewhat differently than carbon dioxide. Nitrogen gas that is used to pour beer has smaller bubbles and does not remain in the beer at the same levels as carbon dioxide. This gives the beer a more flat creamy texture that is pleasant to drink. Guinness™ Irish Stout is always served on a nitrogen tap and anyone who has ever seen or had one of these beers will have had a beer poured on a nitrogen tap.

Pouring Beer

The main task you will undertake with beer is pouring it. You will transfer it from the keg or the bottle to a glass for your guests. It sounds pretty simple. Well, it isn't quite that easy. There are a few subtle factors that you need to take into consideration to make sure that the beer you pour is in the best possible condition to be enjoyed by your guest.

In this section we are going to discuss pouring beer. We will talk about techniques and what you need to look for to make sure that your job is done right.

A proper sized head on a beer is essential to unlocking its flavor potential. This beer has a proper head.

Head is far and away the most important factor in a finished beer. By definition, the head on a glass of beer is the foam that sits on top of the liquid. This area is responsible for most of the flavor a person will taste when they drink the beer. The reason for this is simple. Flavor comes from both taste and smell. They are cooperative senses. In the head of the beer, many of the volatile oils in the beer, especially from the hops, are allowed to evaporate. This creates a vapor that is smelled by the guest at the same time the beer is being tasted in the mouth. This creates a melding of senses. These two sensations together are the flavor of the beer. Without a proper head, a large component of the flavor is missing and the guest will not enjoy the beer nearly as much as they would have otherwise.

When pouring a beer, always leave a head of between .5-1.00 inches above the liquid part of the beer. Many bars and restaurants have rules that set the standard size head for a beer. It is better to have too much head than too little where flavor is concerned.

Most of the beer you will pour will come from a kegged beer and will be poured from a beer tap. There are two kinds of taps that we have talked about. These are the carbon dioxide tap and the nitrogen gas tap. Beer on a nitrogen tap will need time to settle You will need to scoop out excess head and keep filling the glass. Bottled beer will be poured in a style identical to pouring a beer from a carbon dioxide tap.

Instructions For Pouring A Beer

The first step when pouring a beer from a carbon dioxide tap is to bring the glass within a few inches to the tap at a sharp angle like that shown in the picture at right. **Do not allow the tap to touch the glass.** This can break the glass or contaminate it.

Open the tap all the way by pulling it towards you. The beer will pour out. The close proximity and the angle of the glass shorten the fall of the beer and greatly reduce the amount foam that will result.

As the beer fills the glass, gradually reduce the angle of the glass so that eventually the beer is pouring straight into the glass like that shown in the picture to the right.

This has the effect of creating foam as the pour finishes. This is called "coaxing a head". This move will help ensure that the beer has a proper head and the full flavor of the beer can be enjoyed by the guest.

DO NOT simply open a tap and allow the beer to foam into an unangled glass. This will cause the beer to foam and fill the entire glass with beer.

If you pour too much head, do not simply displace it by allowing the tap to run and fill the glass to the appropriate level like the picture. This is very wasteful.

Instead, scoop out the excess head with a spoon and repeat the pouring process with a partially filled glass. If needed, scoop out any excess head a second time.

If for some reason a beer has been sitting and the head has gone flat, you can always re-coax a head by stirring the beer with a cocktail straw. This is not recommended as a standard practice but will work in a pinch.

Increase Your Knowledge

This chapter is by no means designed to be a complete education on the world of beer. The beer industry is a complicated and widely varying set of manufacturers and products that changes almost every day. Just as a nurse or teacher will need to continue their education throughout their career to remain efficient, you will need to do the same as a bartender. There are many ways that you can do this. I will list a few of them here.

Visit The Breweries In Your Area

In 1919 Congress passed the Volstead Act that made alcohol illegal. Prior to this legislation, in most cities, beer had been produced by small craft breweries that served a small geographic area. The Volstead Act forced most of these breweries out of business. The very few breweries that did survive to see the relegalization of alcohol quickly dominated the beer market and grew into the major brewing companies you know today.

In many cases legal obstacles existed that prevented small breweries from brewing and serving their own beers under the same roof. This made small brewing difficult to operate profitably.

In the late seventies and early eighties people who brewed beer at home, as a hobby, and loved the art began to help change these laws. Soon small breweries began to pop up around the country.

The seeds that those home brewers sowed many years ago have blossomed. Today, all over the country you can find small craft breweries. These breweries tend to make small batch specialty beers. Many of these breweries operate pubs where food is served and only their beers are poured. In many cases, these pubs are the only distribution outlet for the beers they brew, although some small breweries have grown large enough to distribute their beers on a national or even international scale.

I strongly recommend that you visit one or many of these small breweries. Frequently, you will be able to sample their range of products for free, if not cheaply. This will greatly increase your knowledge of beer and will make you a better bartender. You will also learn which foods pair with which beers for a more complete meal. Lastly visiting breweries can be a great deal of fun. Take a friend or a date and make a day of it.

Travel The World Without Leaving Home

Great beers are not a product of the United States alone. Many of the best beers in the world are produced elsewhere. Tasting these beers and becoming familiar with their production and characters is another great way to increase your product knowledge and your skill as a bartender.

Many specialty stores that stock exotic foreign beers exist around the country. Find one of these stores in your area and discover what and true English brown, Czech pilsner, Russian stout or Japanese rice beer really taste like. Any bar owner will be impressed with a beer knowledge that spans the globe.

Try Home Brewing

Sometimes the best way to learn about something is to do it. It is no different for beer. As was stated earlier, the beer brewing process is not terribly complicated. Of course, sophisticated computer aided brewing on a massive scale is part of a large brewery's manufacturing process. However, you can achieve very good results with nothing more than a large cooking kettle, a plastic bucket fermenter and some inexpensive bottling equipment.

With the large growth in interest in specialty beers, home brewing supply stores are common in many parts. If one of these outlets is not available in your area, you will certainly find many eager suppliers on the Internet. Try starting out with a guidebook to home brewing and go from there.

Many of the large home brewing supplies will also make brewing equipment available in rented spaces. This way you can take advantage of their cooking kettles and fermenters. This is a great idea if you are living in a small space and do not have the square footage necessary for an operation at home.

Conclusion

Beer can very easily be the most common beverage you will pour as a bartender. You need to be familiar with the process of brewing as well as being able to speak about and describe beer in a clear manner. The buzzwords provided in this chapter will provide you with that ability as well as the short description of the brewing process. Also, know the basic beer types. These were also discussed in this chapter.

Be able to tell a guest which beers are sweet and which will present a crisp and refreshing.

Review Questions

1. What are the three main ingredients in beer?
2. What is a good buzzword to describe an IPA?
3. What is a good buzzword to describe a porter?
4. What are the two common gases that are used to pour beer?
5. Describe the process of pouring a glass of beer.

Answers

1. The three main ingredients in beer are water, grain (usually barley) and hops.

2. Hoppy is a good buzzword to describe an IPA.

3. Malty is a good buzzword to describe a porter.

4. The two common gases used to pour beer are carbon dioxide and nitrogen gas.

5. To pour a glass of beer, hold the glass close to the tap at a sharp angle. Open the tap fully. Allow the glass to fill. Slowly decrease the angle of the glass as it fills. This will coax a proper head.

Chapter 2
Wine

Wine, like beer has been a part of human culture for many thousands of years. If you look at a grape, you will see a grayish, waxy hue to it. This is actually naturally occurring yeast. If the grapes are crushed and the skins allowed to sit in the juice, fermentation will automatically begin. It is not hard to imagine humans, thousands of years ago accidentally discovering this fact and, over the centuries refining the process to create all the varied complex wines we know and appreciate today.

This picture shows Egyptians cultivating grapes and turning them into wine. Winemaking has been a part of human history for thousands of years.

As wine culture and manufacturing are processes that have been evolving and changing for thousands of years, and today make up a vast multibillion dollar international industry, this chapter will not even scratch the surface of the subject. I am not a wine expert and will tell you that right up front. This chapter will deal with only basic wine knowledge that you will need to be able to speak about wine and inform your guests. At the end of this chapter, I will again suggest several methods of continuing your exploration of this subject. It may take you a lifetime to truly understand and appreciate wine, but it is well worth the effort.

The Winemaking Process

The winemaking process is fairly simple. However, there are many steps that can be taken to add different flavor characteristics to the wine.

The process begins with the harvesting of the grapes once their sugar levels have reached a point where they can be easily turned into wine. Wine grapes are grown on specialized farms known as vineyards. The grapes are placed in machinery that strips off the stems. The next step in the process is crushing the grapes. In traditional winemaking, the grapes were crushed manually in an open vat. Modern machinery has simplified this process and today, most grapes are crushed using automatic presses. Depending on the type of wine that is being made, the skins may or may not be allowed to remain in the juice during fermentation. Allowing the skins to remain imparts the red color in finished wine. By controlling the amount of time the skins soak in the juice, as well as the amount of skins in the juice, red grapes can be used to make white wines and a wide range of pink wines. The most famous of these types of wine would be a White Zinfandel.

Wine grapes are cultivated on specialized farms called "vineyards".

The juice and skin mix is then allowed to ferment. This is most often carried out in an open top talk. Again, traditionally, this was carried out in oak barrels. However, these days, many wines are allowed to ferment in plastic and stainless steel tanks. Both of these processes also impart additional flavors to the finished wine.

Unlike beer, wine is allowed to rest for a long period after the fermentation process. This helps to stabilize the flavors in the wine and makes for a more enjoyable finished product. Most commonly, white oak barrels or stainless steel are used to age wine. Only once the aging process is complete will the wine be bottled. After bottling the wine is often allowed to rest again. This allows the flavors in the wine to mature and avoids poorly flavored wine known as "bottle shock".

Wine is commonly aged in white oak barrels like the ones in this picture.

Tasting Wine

Tasting wine is a very important part of wine culture and is essential to truly enjoying and understanding wine. It is also extremely fun to do. Basically, the process is a thorough examination of the wine with all of your senses.

The process is very simple and there are only three things you need to do to properly taste a wine. You need to look at the color of the wine, smell the aroma of the wine and finally taste it.

To examine the color of the wine, tip the glass over something white. Look at the color at the edge of the wine. Is it thick? Thick color density can indicate an older bottle that has bottled aged for a while. Does the color thin out toward the edge of the liquid? This can indicate a high alcohol content. Learn to describe the subtle variations in the colors of the wine in more than just red, white and pink. Words like ruby and crimson are better.

Tipping a glass and studying the colors of the wine are the first steps in tasting.

After the colors of the wine have been examined, it is time to smell the wine. As with beer, the volatile oils in the wine are an absolutely essential component to the wine's true flavor. To help release these aromas, swirl the wine around in the glass. This helps to release the flavors by aerating the wine. The characteristic shape of a wine glass helps to keep these aromas concentrated to make smelling easier. Once you have swirled the wine, stick your nose right into the glass. Don't worry. Everyone else will be doing this as well. What scents can you detect? Fruit aromas are very common. These can include blackberry, apple, strawberry or melon. However, other more exotic and subtle aromas can be present as well. Leather and cheese are examples of these more complex scents. As you continue tasting, your sense of smell will grow stronger and you will be able to detect ever increasing numbers of scents. One word of caution is to watch out for wine that has the smell of wet cardboard. This can indicate a bottle of wine that has gone bad and is unfit for consumption. This wine is not dangerous, only unpleasant to drink. If you smell this, stop tasting and move on.

A good amount of space above the wine in a balloon style wine glass, like this one, will greatly help to release all of the wine's smells.

The last step in the process of wine tasting is to actually taste the wine. This is done by taking a small sip of the wine. Do not swallow it! Hold it in your mouth to start. Slowly tip your face downwards and suck air through the wine into your mouth. This can be a little tricky at first but you will get the hang of it. This again, helps to aerate the wine and release the flavors. Once you have aerated the wine. Swish it around in your mouth. Different parts of your mouth and tongue are sensitive to different types of flavors. For example sweet, salty and tart are all perceived in different areas of the mouth. Swishing the wine in your mouth helps to ensure that you are tasting the full flavor structure of the wine. What do you taste? Don't rush and enjoy the flavor sensation.

Types of Wine

There are four families of wine that we are going to explore in this book. These are red wines, white wine, pink wines, and dessert wines. These families are in turn made up of different varietals and wine styles. The term varietal means wine produced from a single specific type of grape. I am sure that you are already quite familiar with many different vareital names. These include, but are not limited to, merlot, riesling, chardonnay, pinot gris, and pinot noir. In addition to wines that are made from purely one type of grape, there are blended wines which contain wines made form several types of grapes as well as dessert wines that have undergone special conditioning.

Pink Wines

There are no pink grapes. However, the wine markets are full of pink wines. How is this possible? It's simple. Many red wine grapes have clear juices when the grapes are crushed. The color of the grapes lies in the grape's skin. Grapes that posses this quality include Zinfandel and Pinot Noir.

By extracting the juice from grapes of this nature and preventing them from fermenting with their skins, wine makers can actually make Pinot Noir and Zinfandel wines that are just as clear as a Riesling or Chardonnay. By controlling the amount of time the grapes are allowed to ferment with their skins, winemakers can actually "color" their wines from pink to red. This is where pink wines actually come from.

In the wine industry there are two types of pink wines. These are blush and rosé wines. A blush wine is generally a very sweet pink wine. A rosé wine is a wine whose residual sugars have all been turned to alcohol. Rose wines are generally very dry when compared to a blush wine.

Red Wines

Red wine is, simply put, red. This type of wine is produced from grapes varietals whose skins are dark in color. During the fermentation process, these wines are allowed to sit with their skins. These skins add their pigments to the fermentation mix and cause the finished product to have the characteristic blood red color for which red wines are known.

In addition to color, the skins also add tannins to the finished wine. These chemicals are responsible for the dry feeling that is perceptible when drinking red wine. The same puckery feeling one gets from drinking strong black tea is also attributable to tannins. These chemicals are greatly responsible for the sensation and flavor of red wines but can also cause headaches in some people.

Wines that contain tannins can be very helpful in breaking down oils in food and refreshing the palate. This is very nice if you are enjoying a heavy meal that is rich in creams and fats. Examples of foods like this include red meats and cheeses.

Many red wine varietals are cultivated and even more complicated blended red wines are sold in the wine market today. This discussion will cover only the most very basic of red wines that you are likely to see on a wine list in the bar you will work in.

Red wines are traditionally served at room temperature in glasses that have a large enclosed area to trap their aromas. These glasses are often called "balloons".

Merlot

Merlot grapes are characteristic of the Bordeaux region of France. Wine made from these grapes is often mixed with other wines to form blended red wines. This is true of California merlot wines as well. Many brand name blended red wines are a mix of Merlot and Cabernet Sauvignon, although many California wineries also produce a varietal Merlot.

Merlot wines are medium bodied soft wines that are pleasant to drink. Additionally, these wines are low in both tannins and acids. These wines make an excellent suggestion for people looking for a mellow red table wine.

Cabernet Sauvignon

Cabernet Sauvignon is a traditional Bordeaux grape that was developed within the last several hundred years. Wine from Cabernet Sauvignon grapes are commonly blended with Merlot and other varietals to make the classic full bodied red table wines.

Cabernet Sauvignon wine is a full bodied red wine that has strong characteristic aromas of currant. These wines have a high tannin level and are often softened with oak aging which adds more subtle characteristic to the finished wine. Cabernet Sauvignons are an excellent wine pairing with heavy hearty food such as steaks or venison.

Syrah

"Syrah" is the name given to a red grape type that is grown in Northern France. The same grape is grown and used in wine production in Australia and South Africa where it is commonly called "Shiraz". This is simply a regional variant on the name. The finished wines can be called either Syrah or Shiraz.

The wines made from the Syrah grape are full bodied hearty wines. Often these wines have a spicy, peppery character with undertones of leather. These wines are also high in tannins and will result in a puckery sensation.

Pinot Noir

Pinot Noir grapes are a red wine grape that are almost black in color. In point of fact, the name "noir" is the French word for black. Pinot Noir grapes are temperamental in nature and can often be difficult to grow. These wines prefer cooler climates and are grown in Burgundy France, the coastal regions of California and the Pacific Northwest.

Wines made from Pinot Noir grapes are light to medium bodied with subtle fruit flavors. People who enjoy drinking red wine and often get headaches from the tannins may enjoy the trend toward lighter tannin concentrations in Pinot Noir.

Zinfandel

Zinfandel is a red grape that is cultivated almost exclusively in the California wine areas. The red wines made from Zinfandel grapes are generally full bodied in nature with a hearty bouquet.

Zinfandel grapes are also used extensively for the production of White Zinfandels. These wines are made from the uncolored juices of the Zinfandel grape that are allowed to ferment with the grape skins until the desired level of color has been reached.

White Wines

White wines are not actually white in color. They are a family of straw colored, light, crisp and refreshing translucent wines. These wines are produced from grapes that are yellow to light green in color.

As opposed to red wines, white wines are made without allowing the grape skins to ferment with the juice. This prevents any coloring of the wine and also produces a finished wine that is free from tannin. This creates a much lighter wine that is lacking in the dry tannin sensation. This also has the effect of allowing the sweetness and fruit flavors of the finished wine to be much more pronounced. This helps to give white wines their crisp, sweet refreshing flavors that makes them popular, especially in the summer months.

White wines are served cold as a rule. They can be served in the same glass styles as red wines as they too offer aromas that are very enjoyable.

Pinot Gris

Pinot Gris is thought to be a mutant offshoot of the Pinot Noir variety. This grape is generally a grayish blue color leading to the French designation "gris" meaning grey. It is relevant to note that Pinot Gris and Pinot Grigio are the same things whether you are referring to the grape or the wine. Pinot Gris is the French designation and Pinot Grigio is the Italian translation of that name.

Pinot Gris wine is a grayish straw colored white wine. Generally these wines are light and crisp in character. This makes Pinot Gris an excellent wine during the summer months or with lighter food.

Riesling

Riesling is a white grape that is popular in German and Eastern French wine production. Riesling grapes are also cultivated heavily in the California growing areas as well as Australia and South Africa.

Riesling wines can run a large range of flavors from crisp refreshing and low alcohol white table wines to very sweet wines that are very nice as a dessert wine.

Sauvignon Blanc

Sauvignon Blanc is a white wine grape that is commonly associated with Bordeaux France and is cultivated a great deal in New Zealand, South Africa and North America. This wine is generally not oak aged and is referred to as a Fume Blanc when oak aging has taken place.

Words that are often associated with Sauvignon Blanc are crisp and refreshing and the wine displays strong fruit flavors. These qualities make Sauvignon Blanc and excellent lunch time wine and one that will quench any thirst on a hot summer afternoon. Sauvignon Blanc, being a light wine, is easily paired with lighter foods such as fish.

Chardonnay

Chardonnay is the most widely cultivated grape in the world. Anywhere that wine is produced; you will find the grape being heavily cultivated and many wineries producing a chardonnay wine. In fact, this grape is often used as a pioneer species in newer wine areas because of it forgiving nature and ease of cultivation.

Strong oak flavors are characteristic of chardonnay wines as is a buttery flavor. These traits are due to the wine making process of fermenting the wine in oak barrels. However, chardonnay wines can also be produced without these qualities and instead offer a wide range of strong fruit essences.

In recent years there has been a bit of a backlash towards chardonnay. Many wine drinkers and the wine market in general have developed the term "ABC" meaning "Anything But Chardonnay". Many in these circles see Chardonnays as undercutting the artistic and local process of winemaking and leading wine to the mass market production techniques that dominate with beer and distilled spirits.

Sparkling White Wines

Many white wines are carbonated by a second round of fermentation in the bottle. The yeast consumes the remaining or added sugar in the bottles and creates carbon dioxide which dissolves into the wine. Legend has it that a Benedictine monk who was making wine discovered this process and gave the gift of bubbly wines to the world.

Grapes that are commonly used to make sparkling white wines are Chardonnay and Pinot Noir. California sparkling Pinot Noirs have greatly increasing in popularity throughout the world.

While sparkling white wines can be made in any wine growing region, only wines specifically made in the Champagne region of France can properly be called "Champagne".

Fortified Wines

Fortified wines are a mixture of a sweet base wine and a stronger alcohol, usually a brandy. This has the effect of creating a stronger sweet wine. These wines are traditional wines of both Spain and Portugal.

Because of their increased strength fortified wines are served in a much smaller portion than regular wines. Also, fortified wines are served in special cordial glasses.

Fortified wines are served in smaller portions in specialty cordial glasses.

Port

Port is a fortified wine that is a specialty of Portugal. Port wine is fortified during the fermentation process. This ends fermentation and preserves a good part of the sweetness of the wine. This wine also has a very strong sweet raisin flavor to it. Port is an excellent dessert wine but also pairs well with cheese. Ports are also used in cooking quite a bit.

Madeira

Madeira is an island chain in the Atlantic off the coast of Portugal and Spain. These islands have a long history of winemaking. During the colonization of the New World, Madeira wine was often shipped to the Spanish colonies. During transport, the wine was subjected to a long period of heating and cooling known as "baking". This gave the wine a unique and pleasing character. Today this process is repeated using artificial means, but still creates the same result. Madeira is also used a great deal in cooking where it is a frequent ingredient in cream reduction sauces.

Sherry

Sherry is a traditional fortified wine of Spain. Sherry differs from port in that it is allowed to complete fermentation before the wine is fortified. This gives the wine a complex dry character.

Sherry is always a blended wine. Using a centuries old technique known as the solera system, wine from past vintages is blended with new production wine to create the finished blended wines.

<u>Opening a Bottle of Wine</u>

When a guest orders a bottle of wine, you will need to open the bottle in front of them. This is a traditional step that assures the guest that the bottle of wine has not been opened prior to their ordering it. Also during this ritual, the guest has the option to return the bottle if they discover that the wine is "corked". Corked is a term that means the wine has gone bad from a improperly sealed cork. By some estimates as many as 10% of all bottles of wine are corked.

A wine key suitable for tableside opening includes a corkscrew as well as a small knife for cutting the foil on the wine bottle.

After you have gotten the bottle of wine, the first step in the opening process is to present the label of the bottle to the guest. This is a check to make sure that you have grabbed the right bottle and the guest has not ordered the wrong bottle by mistake. Sometimes there can be confusion during ordering. If you have grabbed the wrong bottle or the guest has ordered the wrong bottle, correct the problem.

After you have assured you have the right bottle, place a glass in front of each guest that will be sharing the bottle. Now, cut the foil with the small knife on the wine opener. Cut the foil below the rim on the wine bottle's neck. Traditionally lead foil was used and cutting the foil a good distance away from where the wine would pour helped to prevent contamination and lead poisoning. Today lead is not used in the foils.

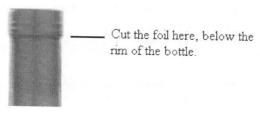
Cut the foil here, below the rim of the bottle.

Cut the foil of a wine bottle just below the lip of the bottle.

A corkscrew is used to pull the cork from a bottle of wine.

To open the bottle, remove the cork. To do this, place the point of the corkscrew in the very center of the cork. Begin twisting. Do not stop until all of the turns of the corkscrew are in the cork. Then place the fulcrum on the lip of the bottle as shown in the photo. Use the corkscrew as a lever to gently remove the cork. There should be no sound as the cork is removed.

Once the bottle is open, pour a small taste for the person who ordered the bottle. Allow them to taste the wine. Once they have done so, ask if the wine is acceptable. This is the point where they can refuse the wine. If they do, repeat the process with another bottle of wine of their choosing. If they accept the wine, ask if they would like you to pour the wine for them. If they accept the offer, pour a glass for everyone who is sharing the bottle. Start with the person to the right of the one who ordered the bottle and move around the table. The person who receives wine last should be the one who ordered the bottle.

There is a little trick to pouring a glass of wine. Hold the bottle in your right hand and begin pouring. When you are getting close to being done filling the glass, rotate your hand slowly in a clockwise fashion at the same time you tip the bottle up. This will elegantly terminate the flow of wine and make sure that no wine dribbles onto the glass's base or on the tablecloth.

If the guests declines the offer to pour them a glass, place the bottle on the table or bar along with the cork. You are finished.

If you are opening a bottle of sparkling wine, the process is slightly different. The difference lies in how you open the bottle. Sparkling wines do not require a corkscrew. The pressure from the carbonation will allow you to remove the cork with your hand. To do so, untwist and remove the wire frame that restrains the cork. This is shown in the picture below. **When opening a bottle of sparkling wine, always point it away from anyone. The cork can fly out and injure people if handled improperly.** Place a towel over the cork and slowly twist while pulling. The cork should come out easily. Watch out as the wine may foam a bit. At this point, continue the wine presentation process the same as before.

Be careful when opening champagne as the cork is under pressure.

Wine Serving Sizes

In the United States, six ounces is considered a standard pour for a glass of red, pink or white wine. Wine is packaged for the international market and the metric system is used. A standard bottle of wine is 750 milliliters or a little over 25 ounces. That means that you should be able to pour four glasses of wine from a single bottle and have just a little left over.

Fortified wines, because of their higher alcohol content are served in three ounce portions. This has roughly the same amount of alcohol as is present in a six ounce glass of unfortified wine.

Wine Buzzwords

Just like beer, a list of buzzwords to describe wine will be very helpful to you when you start bartending. Again, these words help convey very abstract ideas to a guest regarding the flavors of the wine. You should read this list carefully and become very familiar with these words.

Fruity – This word is used to describe the sweet flavor of fruit in the wine. Examples of these flavors are apple, melon and strawberries. This is a good word to use with sweet blush wines.

Sweet – A wine can be described as sweet when there is a high level of remaining sugars in the wine. This is a great descriptor for many Rieslings.

Dry – Use the word "dry" to describe wines that lack sweetness. Dry wines complement food well. A typical dry wine is a Chardonnay.

Crisp – "Crisp" is a good word to use with wines that are refreshing and have a pleasing acidity or tartness.

Full Bodied – Use this descriptor to discuss wines that have rich flavors and are high in alcohol. This descriptor is best applied to red wines.

Rich – "Rich" is a descriptor often applied to red wines. It is used to impart heavy, full bodied flavor and strong flavors such as currant or blackberry.

Light- Light is a descriptor that is used to describe wines that are low in acidity.

Oakey – Wines that have been aged in oak barrels are often described as being "oakey". This descriptor is used to describe the buttery textures in the resulting wine and higher tannin levels.

Wine Continuing Education

As I mentioned in the opening paragraph of this chapter, I am not an expert on wine and I do not pretend to be. In writing this chapter, it was not my intention to create a thorough and definitive guide to wines. The goal was simply to give you the basic knowledge of wine you would need in order to work efficiently as a bartender. However, to learn more about wines, there are many steps you can take. A few of these will be discussed in the following pages.

Read

Visiting your local library or book store is a great place to continue your wine education. There are whole volumes in either one of these locations that are dedicated exclusively to the subject of wine. These books will discuss specific manufacturing processes and the various wine growing regions. Additionally, there are many types of wines that I have not mentioned in this book. Names like viognier, grenache, claret, Chianti and gewürztraminer come up less often than the wines I have mentioned so far, but these types of wine will be discussed in books dedicated to only wine. You can also learn about the various wine growing regions of the world and the specifics of the wines these areas offer.

Visit a Winery

Visiting a winery is another really good way to experience wine culture and increase your knowledge. This can be a little hard if there is no wine grown where you live. However, wine is produced all over the world and a trip to wine country is always a very pleasant trip.

In the United States, wine is produced in the Northeast or along the Pacific coast with major areas of cultivation in California and the Northwest. A trip to anyone of these locales can be very rewarding. Often, there are charter tour groups that will take you around to various wineries in these areas and allow you to taste without having to worry about driving afterwards.

If you have a taste for the exotic, on your next trip to South Africa, Chile, Australia, New Zealand or Europe, visit the wine producing areas of these regions as well.

Taste Wine

If wine is not produced in your area or you cannot get away to visit a winery, there is still hope. Anywhere in the United States, you will find wine shops, wine bars and even wine clubs. These are businesses and social groups dedicated specifically to the tasting and enjoyment of wine. These resources are an excellent place to start with your exploration of all the facets of wine culture.

Find a wine shop and stop in. Tell them that you are new to wine tasting, or if you are a more experienced wine enthusiast, tell them what you like and do not care for. They will be only too happy to help you make selections and introduce you to new wineries and vintages that you may have missed up to this point. They may also be able to help you experience some really great wines that will not break your wallet. These people are the experts and ignoring them would be a real mistake.

Wine clubs are formal or informal social groups that meet at regular intervals. These people love wine and love to talk about it. They will get together, everybody bringing a bottle of some kind, and everyone shares and tastes the various wine selections. This can be a great way to taste a wide range of wines, learn a lot and meet some really great people in the bargain. Additionally, these gatherings are a lot of fun.

Conclusion

Wine will be a very common drink that you will be pouring in any bartending situation. You need to be familiar with it. This chapter will give you the basic knowledge that you need, but strongly consider some of the continuing education ideas that were just mentioned. These will help you better understand what you are pouring and will make you a better bartender.

Know the wines that were mentioned in this chapter as well. These are basic wine types that you will find in just about any bar you will ever work in. These are the wines Americans always want. As I have hinted already, there are many other wine types as well and you will most likely see them at some point. When you do encounter a new wine, always taste it. This will most likely be permitted by your employer as it will help you to sell it. Also get to know a little about the wine and the grape type. Information is always helpful and the more you have the better at your new career you will be.

Review Questions

1. Name two of the white wines mentioned in this chapter.

2. Name two of the red wines that were discussed in this chapter.

3. How are blush (pink) wines made?

4. Why do you not fill a glass of wine all the way to the top?

5. What is a fortified wine? Name one.

6. How many six ounce glasses of wine are in a 750 ml bottle?

Answers

1. Chardonnay, Sauvignon Blanc, Riesling, Pinot Gris

2. Zinfandel, Pinot Noir, Syrah, Cabernet Sauvignon, Merlot

3. Blush wines are made from the clear juice of red grapes. The color is added to the wine by allowing the juice to ferment with the red skins until the desired level of pink has been attained.

4. It is important to leave air above the wine in a glass so that the scents of the wine can be trapped in the glass for smelling. This is an important part of the tasting process.

5. A fortified wine is a wine to which another alcohol (usually brandy) has been added. This raises the alcohol content, helps to preserve the wine and is used to manipulate the flavors of the wine.

6. There are about four six ounce glasses in a 750 ml bottle.

Chapter 3
Distilled Spirits

Alcohol and water, which are both liquids, boil at different temperatures. Alcohol boils at a much lower temperature than water. By raising a solution of alcohol and water to the boiling point of alcohol, you can boil off the alcohol while leaving the water in a liquid state. If you capture the vapor produced from boiling and cool it to the point where it becomes a liquid again, you will have a solution that has a much higher alcohol content than the solution you started with. This is the basic process of distillation. By repeating this process several times, you can produce a solution that is almost pure alcohol. These solutions are called "distilled spirits" or just "spirits".

To start the process of distillation you need a mixture that already contains alcohol. Distillation does not create alcohol. Only yeast, through fermentation can create alcohol. Distillation only concentrates the alcohol. The process begins by fermenting a mixture of fruit or grain with water and yeast. This mixture is known as the "mash". With moonshine, this mash can be a simple mixture of refined sugar and water. Once the mash is done fermenting and all the sugar has been converted to alcohol, the mash is ready to be distilled. It is placed in the distillery and the alcohol is concentrated in the manner already described.

Distilled spirits are manufactured in large cooking kettles know as distilleries. The alcohol is trapped and cooled to make a finished spirit.

Distilled spirits are a very complex and varying group of alcoholic beverages. They can be made from many, many different ingredients including wines, potatoes, grains, and even cacti. A single type of distilled sprit, such as tequila, can be aged in many different ways making distinctly different finished products. Some spirits are made only in specific regions of the globe. Scotch is an example of this. Some spirits are not aged at all, but are raw alcohol that is infused with different fruits to create very pleasant flavors. In this chapter, we are going to explore the basic types of distilled sprits. This information will be essential in the next chapter when we discuss mixed drinks.

Long term barrel aging is a common process used with many distilled sprits. The barrels are often stored in large warehouses like this one.

Whiskeys

A whiskey is any distilled spirit made from grain. This is usually barely, corn, or rye. Once the mash has been distilled, the raw spirits are aged in oak barrels. This has the effect of coloring the liquor to a deep caramel color as well as allowing the whiskey to take on strong and pronounced flavors from the wood barrels.

The barrels used in whiskey making are often barrels that have been used to age sherry or other wines. Burning the barrel's interior is also a common practice with Bourbon style whiskeys.

Whiskey is the traditional distilled spirit of Scotland and Ireland. These whiskeys are often distinguished from others by being called Scotch or Irish whiskey. However, due to the migrations of the Scotch and Irish during the peopling of the Americas, whiskeys are also now produced in Canada and the United States. These whiskeys are usually called Canadian whiskey, rye, or Bourbon.

Scotch Whiskey

Scotch whiskey is the traditional distilled spirit of Scotland. Scotch is made from barley as a rule. Also, the barley is traditionally malted before it is ground and fermented. During the malting process, the barley is dried using a peat fire.

Peat bogs like this one, are common throughout Scotland and Ireland. These bogs provide inexpensive fuel that gives Scotch whiskey its distinct flavor.

Peat is a biomass fuel source pulled from peat bogs. These bogs are really just acidic swamps that have been building up for thousands of years. These bogs have provided a cheap and convenient fuel source for the people of Scotland for about as long. The peat fire adds a distinctive flavor to the finished whiskey that is often described as "peaty".

There are two common types of Scotch whiskey that you will find. These are single malt and blended whiskey. A single malt whiskey is made from a single type of malted barley. Blended whiskeys are made from several single malt whiskeys that are made using different malt types. These blends are produced to create more complex and pleasing flavors in the finished whiskey.

Scotland is very protective of its Scotch industry. As such it has enacted laws that define what can and cannot be called Scotch whiskey. These include that the liquor must be distilled from barley, must be aged in oak, <u>in Scotland,</u> cannot be aged less than three years, and cannot have any additives other than water.

Irish Whiskey

Irish whiskey is another style of whiskey. This whiskey is produced exclusively in Ireland. Many people think that Irish whiskey and Scotch whiskey are the same thing. This is not true, although there are similarities.

To begin with, Irish whiskey is not produced using peat. This means that Irish whiskey is lacking in the earthy, peaty flavor that is characteristic of Scotch whiskey.

Irish whiskey is also almost exclusively sold as a blended whiskey. There are of course exceptions to this rule, but single malt Irish whiskeys are much less common.

Canadian Whiskey

Canadian whiskeys are whiskeys that are produced in Canada. These whiskeys are almost always a blended whiskey. Canadian whiskeys are often made from a number of grain types including barley, corn and rye.

Canadian whiskey was imported in large quantities into the United States during Prohibition due to the long, lightly guarded border. Many Canadian distilleries turned a blind eye to the fact that their whiskey was to be smuggled into the United States. Today, Americans still love Canadian whiskeys and you will definitely be pouring them as a bartender.

Bourbon

Bourbon whiskey is a traditional American whiskey. Bourbons, like Canadian whiskeys, are generally a blended spirit. This whiskey style is produced in large quantities in America today with its production being centered in the states of Kentucky and Tennessee. Many whiskeys are sold as either "Tennessee Whiskey" or "Kentucky Whiskey". These are distinct styles of Bourbon whiskey that take into consideration where the whiskey is made. This is similar to the distinction between Scotch and Irish Whiskey.

Bourbon whiskeys are often charcoal filtered whiskeys that are aged in new oak barrels. These barrels are often sold to Scotch distilleries after their use in Bourbon production to be used for aging Scotch.

Also under United States law, any whiskey labeled as Bourbon whiskey must be produced using a mash made from at least 51% corn and aged to a minimum of two years. These laws are similar to Scottish laws and are used to protect the American whiskey industry by ensuring its quality.

Rye Whiskey

Rye whiskey is a whiskey that is made from a mash that is a majority of rye grain. Pure rye whiskeys are not especially common these days and you will be hard pressed to find one in many bars.

<u>Rum</u>

When Europeans first began to colonize the Caribbean Islands, they began to experiment with various crops to increase the profits of the colonies. One of the most lucrative crops that they planted was sugarcane. Refined sugar was highly sought in Europe. This plant, that could be processed to form white sugar quickly spread to many of the islands in the region.

Sugarcane processing at the time was wasteful and many sugary byproducts resulted from the treatment of the cane. Molasses was chief among these byproducts. Colonists soon began to experiment with the molasses and quickly learned that they could ferment and distill the molasses. This was the birth of rum. Rum was viewed as a profitable secondary product of sugarcane and also spread throughout the region.

Sugarcane fields like this one are common throughout the tropics. Molasses from the sugarcane is the main ingredient in a rum mash.

Rum is often associated with pirates and the British Navy, but it is also a very popular liquor for mixed drinks, especially very sweet fruity drinks. Rum is a wonderful liquor during the Summer months or anywhere it is hot. Rum comes in several different varieties, but is rarely drunk straight. Instead, almost all rum drinks actually try to hide the rum in a fruit juice of some kind or with other strong flavors like mint in a mojito.

Light or White Rum

White rum is a neutral form of rum that is not aged at all. This rum is taken directly from the distillery and is bottled. This rum is an excellent rum for mixing and is used in most mixed drinks that involve rum from a rum and cola, to a pina colada or daiquiri.

This type of rum is produced all over the Caribbean region and has little to no flavor other than sweetness.

Gold Rum

Gold rum is another popular type of rum produced in the Caribbean. This type of rum is aged in barrels made from oak or other types of wood. These barrels may be recycled barrels that have been used to make whiskey. This type of rum is often aged for at least three years. This has the effect of coloring the rum to a golden color and allowing it to take on additional flavors from the barrels. This process also tends to mellow the rum. Caramel colors are often added to gold rums. This adds additional sweetness and assures that the finished product is a dark amber in color.

Dark Rum

Dark rum is a rum style that is heavily associated with Jamaica. This type of rum is produced by long aging in barrels that are heavily charred. This creates a rum that has pronounced and complex flavors and is the preferred rum for sipping, if one is so inclined. Dark rums are also colored and flavored with caramel and molasses. This creates a rum that is almost black in color.

Dark rums are often mixed with other rum styles in drinks like Hurricanes and Mai Tais. Often this type of liquor is used as a finishing float, although some guests will prefer a rum and cola made with dark rum. Dark rum is also the best type of rum used for rum punches.

151 Rum

151 rum is rum that has a much higher alcohol content than normal rum. Normal rums are generally about 80 proof or 40% alcohol. 151 rum is actually an "overproof" rum that is more than 75% alcohol. This rum type is actually strong enough to burn. In fact, this is one of this liquor's most valuable features. This type of rum is often used in flaming drinks such as a Spanish Coffee. Burning rum is used to caramelize sugar on the rims of glasses as well as heat them.

Whenever you are lighting 151 rum on fire, use extreme caution. This burning liquid can cause burns as well as additional fires if not handled properly.

Spiced or Flavored Rums

Spiced rums are rums that have had spices and other flavorings added to them. Examples of flavors that are added to these rums are vanilla, nutmeg and allspice. These rums are very popular in hot drinks in the winter. They are also frequently mixed with cola.

Spiced rums are generally gold in color. This color can either be from the use of an aged gold rum or from the addition of caramel coloring to a white rum.

Flavored rums are generally white rums that have tropical fruit flavors added to them. Common fruit flavors are coconut and pineapple. These rums are great mixed with fruit juices and other tropical mixers.

Gin

The Dutch were the first to distill gin and the spirit quickly spread across the channel to England as well. This liquor was very inexpensive to make and quickly became a popular drink among the poor. As the English and Dutch began to colonize the tropics, gin went with them. Gin was (and still is) mixed with tonic water that contains an anti-malarial medicine to help ward of the deadly disease.

Juniper is an evergreen, aromatic piney shrub that is common in both Europe and North America. The berries of the juniper plant are the main flavor in gin.

Gin is made by taking a high proof neutral spirit (lacking any flavor) and mixing in juniper berries and other exotic tropical ingredients and redistilling the mix. The result is a spirit that is infused with the juniper and other ingredients. Gin as a rule is never aged and as such is always clear.

Gin is a popular sipping liquor. It is often drunk with only a little additive as in a gin martini or as a gin and tonic. Gin is, but less often, drunk with juices and other mixers.

London Dry Gin

London dry gin is the classic gin. It is most commonly 80 proof as a finished product. Like all gins, London dry gin is flavored with juniper as a rule along with other tropical spices and botanicals. Also, like all gins London dry gin is never aged.

London dry gins are the best gins to use for making mixed cocktails with gin. The more subtle flavors of a London dry can be mixed well and will not dominate the finished cocktail.

Holland Style Gin

Holland style gins do not vary too much from London dry gins except in the strength of the juniper flavors. Holland style gins have an extremely potent flavor that makes them difficult to mix into cocktails. The reason for this is the juniper flavor will always dominate the finished product no matter what it is mixed with. Dutch gins would make the best sipping gin or a very nice martini. Because of the difficulty in mixing a Holland style gin, they are considerably less common than London dry gins.

Fruit Infused Gin

Gin can also be infused with other ingredients to create sweet and fruit infused gins. The classic example of this style is Sloe Gin. Sloe Gin is a sweet red liquor that is relatively low in alcohol content. This sweet liquor is used in tropical mixers such as an Alabama Slammer or a Sloe Gin Fizz.

Other types of fruit infused gins are becoming increasingly popular. Common flavors are lime, raspberry or orange. These gins make excellent mixers and will only increase in popularity as people become better acquainted with them.

Vodka

Vodka is the traditional spirit of Eastern Europe, including but not limited to, Russia, Finland, Sweden, Poland, Lithuania and the Ukraine. Vodka has been produced in these countries for centuries and is deeply interwoven into the cultures of these regions.

Vodka is a clear, odorless and tasteless alcoholic beverage in its basic state. Vodka is simply the high proof product of distillation without any finishing. It is never aged and is most often bottled at 80 proof. In the 19th century it was decided that this ratio of alcohol to water was ideal for sipping and it has stayed that way ever since.

Vodka can be made by distilling any mash that contains alcohol. The mash can be made from potatoes, grain, or fruits, but potatoes and grain are the most common ingredients in commercial mashes.

Grains like wheat supply the bulk of a vodka mash especially in the United States.

Although vodka is closely associated with Eastern Europe and is produced and consumed in large quantities there, many very popular vodka brands are manufactured in France, the Netherlands, England, Japan and the United States where vodka is also consumed in large quantities.

The only two commercial "styles" of vodka are potato and grain vodka. Although many drinkers express a preference for one type over another, there is little, if any difference.

Vodka is an excellent sipping alcohol. As I have already stated, it has no flavor or smell and is great on the rocks or mixed into a cocktail. Smooth, quality vodka is a real treat to sip!

Infused Vodka

Infused vodkas are where vodka really differentiate and take on many different flavors. Because vodka is a neutral spirit in its pure form, it can be infused with any flavor imaginable. Common favors are lemon, orange, vanilla, and raspberry. However, more exotic flavors like chili peppers, cherries, ginger, lemongrass, currant and cranberry are very common as well. These exotically flavored spirits make excellent cocktails. For example, chili pepper vodka goes great in a Bloody Mary and you could not make a Lemondrop without citrus flavored vodka. In fact, you can infuse your own vodka with whatever flavor you find appealing simply by soaking that type of fruit or vegetable in the vodka. The high alcohol content of the vodka will act as a preservative. Many bars even offer house infused exotically flavored vodkas as a specialty to draw in guests.

Tequila

It is hard to think of Mexico without thinking about tequila. This classic liquor is intimately associated with Mexico and has been produced in that country in large amounts for several hundred years.

When the Spanish arrived in Mexico in 1519, they found the native peoples drinking a fermented drink made from agave. This drink was called pulque. Pulque is a white liquid that is still popular in Mexico, although hard to find in the United States. Eventually, the Spanish experimented with distilling pulque near the town of Tequila and the liquor we know today was born.

Tequila is not produced from a grain or a fruit. Tequila is still produced from a mash made from the agave plant. The agave plant is a fleshy succulent, not unlike an aloe plant. This succulent grows abundantly in Mexico and the Southwest United States. By pressing the plant and extracting the sticky sap, one has a substance that can be easily fermented and distilled.

In the last few decades, tequila has achieved a popular status similar to scotch and cognac. Where once, in the United States, tequila was a liquor for shots and margaritas only, it is now savored by connoisseurs and sipped in brandy snifters by people with discerning and discriminating palates. This has dramatically increased the demand and consequently the price of tequila in recent years. This problem has been compounded by agave plant diseases in the last decade as well.

Agave plants like this one are used in the production of tequila.

There are three popular type of tequila. These are blanco, reposado and anejo.

Blanco Tequila

Blanco is the Spanish word for "white" and this word is commonly used to describe tequila that is fresh from the distillery and has undergone no aging. The Spanish word for silver, "plata" is also commonly used. In English blanco tequila is also called "silver tequila". It is common for inexpensive gold colored tequilas to be blanco tequilas that are colored with caramel coloring.

Reposado Tequila

Reposado is the Spanish word for "rested" and is used to describe tequila that has been allowed to mellow in oak barrels for at least two months. Like other distilled sprits, tequila mellows in the barrels and takes on the flavors and colors from the wood. This makes for more complex flavors and a smoother drink overall. In the United States, reposado tequila is often called gold tequila.

Anejo Tequila

Tequila that has been aged in oak barrels for a year or more is known as anejo tequila. This type of tequila is the best tequila to sip or take as a shot, although many people prefer this type of tequila in a margarita as well. This type of tequila is naturally colored by the aging process and the addition of caramel is rare with anejo tequila.

Brandy

Brandy is a distilled spirit that is usually made from grapes; however, it is not uncommon to find brandies made from other fruits as well. Brandy is closely associated with France, but in reality brandy is made all over Europe and the world as well.

Cognac and Armagnac are special types of French Brandy that, like Champagne are named after the regions where they are produced. California in recent decades has also begun to produce high qaulity brandies that can stand up proudly to their European counterparts.

Brandy is a classic sipping or after dinner drink. Often accompanied by a cigar this liquor is a true pleasure to experience.

Brandies are commonly aged in oak, although some styles are served without any aging. Also, brandies are almost always blended by master distillers to create rich, complex and pleasing flavors. The mixing process will often include brandies that have been produced over many years being combined in one bottle.

Brandy is sometimes mixed in cocktails like a sidecar, however most brandy is enjoyed neat as a sipping cordial. Brandy is also the classic after dinner drink and is often very pleasant with dessert or cigars.

V.S. Brandy

V.S. Brandy is a distinction given to brandies that are made from grapes and are aged in oak barrels for a minimum of three years. The term V.S. is actually short for 'Very Special".

V.S.O.P. Brandy

V.S.O.P. is another distinction given to grape brandies that are aged a minimum of five years. This designation is short for "Very Special Old Pale".

X.O. Brandy

X.O. Brandy is grape brandy that has been aged more than six years. This designation is short for "Extra Old".

Grappa Style Brandy

Grappa is an Italian style brandy that is served without any aging. This brandy is often made from the leftover skins from wine production. It will have a spicy or peppery flavor. Since grappa is not allowed to age, there is almost no mellowing to the spirit. Many first time grappa drinkers will describe grappa as "harsh".

Fruit Brandy

In reality, brandy is any distilled spirit made from fruit. Most of the time, this fruit is the grape. However, any fruit can be used. Apples, pears, and blackberries are commonly used.

Additionally, unaged brandies are mixed with sweet fruit juices to create low alcohol, syrupy sweet liquors that are called brandies as well. Cherry brandy is a common example of this style of distilled spirit.

Cordials

Cordials are a family of sweet, syrupy lower alcohol content, distilled spirits. These liquors are often around 20% alcohol by volume (40 proof). These liquors are generally used as mixers for cocktails and are not frequently drunk on their own. Get to know these liquors as they will be essential in Chapter 5 when we discuss mixing drinks.

Triple Sec – Triple sec will be the most common cordial that you use. It is added to almost any cocktail with juice in it. This is a sweet, clear orange liquor that is made from the dried peels of oranges and distilled three times. The name "triple sec" are the French words for "triple" and "dry".

Coffee Liquor – Coffee liqueur is a mixture of coffee and neutral spirits. Additional flavors are also added. These flavors always include vanilla. This liqueur is commonly used in many hot drinks as well as cold drinks like White and Black Russians.

Irish Cream – Irish creams are a mixture of Irish whiskey with cream and flavors. Common flavors are coffee and vanilla. This liqueur style is common in many drinks and is often consumed on its own over ice or with a single mixer like coffee.

Blue Curacao – The Caribbean island of Curacao is actually part of the Netherlands. During the colonial period, Dutch settlers began to distill an orange liqueur from the peels of the bitter oranges that grow naturally on the island. Today blue Curacao is made all over the world and is used to color drinks blue as well as add an orange flavor. This spirit is used in drinks like an A.M.F. and a Blue Hawaii.

Crème de cacao – Crème de cacao is a chocolate liqueur. This liqueur comes in either a light, clear variety or a dark brown color. Light crème de cacao is useful for chocolate martinis, while dark crème de cacao is useful for drinks like a Coffee Nudge.

Crème de Menthe – Crème de menthe is a green peppermint liqueur that is good for adding a green color to drinks as well as peppermint flavor. This liqueur is good for making drinks like a Grasshopper.

Hazelnut Liqueur – Hazelnut liqueur is a syrupy liqueur that has a strong hazelnut taste. This flavor is great with chocolate as well for making rich and decadent hot cocktails like a Monastery, which is a mix of hazelnut liqueur, Irish cream and coffee. This liqueur also makes great shots like a Chocolate Cake.

Cinnamon Schnapps – Cinnamon schnapps is a cinnamon flavored liqueur. This liqueur is often requested as a shot, but can be used in cocktails like an Oatmeal Cookie as well.

Peach Schnapps – Peach schnapps is a peach flavored liqueur. This liqueur is a great mixer with orange juice and can be used to make Fuzzy Navels or a Miami Iced Tea. Peach schnapps can also be used to make shot drinks like a Brain Hemorrhage.

Peppermint Schnapps – Peppermint schnapps is a clear mint liqueur. This liqueur is best used when you want to add mint flavor to a drink without the green color of crème de menthe. This liqueur is good for drinks like a Peppermint Patty which is a mix of peppermint schnapps and hot chocolate.

Sour Apple Liqueur – Sour apple has become a very popular flavor in recent years. This liqueur is good for adding a refreshing, crisp fruit flavor to drinks or for blending with apple vodka to make a Sour Apple Martini.

Raspberry/Currant Liqueur – Raspberry and currant liqueurs add a sweet syrupy berry flavor to drinks. These liqueurs are good for making Raspberry Kamikazes and Black Pearls.

Butterscotch Schnapps – Butterscotch schnapps is a liqueur that is flavored to taste like butterscotch candy. This liqueur makes a good addition to hot drinks or is used to make shot drinks like a Buttery Nipple.

Anisette/Licorice Liqueur – Licorice liqueurs are common in many bars but are not used in many cocktails. The exception to this rule is a Root Beer Float. Anisette is a type of licorice liqueur that is a traditional Italian cordial. Anisette is often drunk on its own.

Melon Liqueur – Melon liqueur is a great summer flavor to add to drinks and blends well with juice. Melon liqueur is commonly mixed with sour mix to add tartness or in summer coolers like and Electric Watermelon.

Sambuca and Ouzo – Sambuca and Ouzo are Italian and Greek liquors respectively. In essence these are really the same liquor made in different parts of the world. This liquor style is a clear, syrupy licorice flavored liqueur that turns white when it is mixed with water. This liqueur style is popular as a shot on special occasions like weddings or as a sipper. Always serve sambuca in the traditional style with three coffee beans in it.

Amaretto – Amaretto is a sweet Italian style liqueur made from almonds and is often flavored with other exotic spices. This liqueur is often consumed on the rocks or in juice cocktails where it adds a pleasing almond sweetness. This spirit is also good for cooking.

Conclusion

Study this chapter carefully. As a bartender, you will be required to have a thorough working knowledge of spirits in order to properly serve you guests. Not only will you need to know the differences between various types of tequilas, but you will need to know how these liquors mix to form cocktails. We will be discussing how to mix these spirits with each other and with mixers in a subsequent chapter.

Review Questions

1. What is peat and how is it used in the process of making scotch?

2. What is a neutral spirit? Name an example of a neutral spirit.

3. What is pulque? How is tequila made from pulque?

4. What is triple sec? How is triple sec used in the bar?

5. What is the main flavor in gin? What is the difference between a London Dry and a Holland style gin?

Answers

1. Peat is a fuel source that is extracted from peat bogs which are common in Scotland. This fuel is used in the fires that dry the barley malt used to make scotch. This adds an earthy flavor to finished scotch.

2. A neutral spirit is a distilled spirit without any flavor. Vodka is an example of a neutral spirit. Neutral sprits are commonly infused with flavors to make other types of liquors like gin or coffee liqueurs.

3. Pulque is a fermented drink made from the sap of the agave plant. Pulque is distilled to make blanco tequila. The tequila can then be aged to make reposado or anejo tequila.

4. Triple sec is an orange flavored cordial made from dry orange peels. Triple sec is used in many cocktail like Lemondrops and Sidecars as a mixer.

5. The main flavor in gin is juniper. Holland style gin differs from London Dry gin in that it has a very stong juniper flavor that makes it unsuitable for use in cocktails where it is mixed with other liquors. Holland style gin will make a great martini.

Chapter 4
Bartending Equipment & Terms

When I was first trained to bartend, the first thing my trainer and I did was take a tour behind the bar. We needed to make sure that we spoke a common language regarding the bar. That way, I could understand what I was being told. If I tell you to muddle two limes and you do not know what a muddler is, this can be a problem. To make sure that we are on the same page, this chapter introduces you to the tools of your new trade and will explain terms that you are likely to encounter in any bartending environment you will work in.

Glasses

Without glasses, you are out of business. They are one of the most important items that you have behind a bar. When you run out of them, things get pretty rough, pretty fast. In this book, you will encounter many terms like "bucket" and "cocktail". These refer to glasses. All of the glass types that will be referenced in this book are summarized in the following pages. Study them and know them by heart.

Shot Glass

A shot glass, as its name implies is designed to hold only one shot of liquor. Often, you will find these glasses with marks on them to indicate the exact fill mark on the glass when it is filled with 1.5 ounces of liquid.

Pint Glass

A pint glass is a beer glass that holds 16 ounces of beer. These glasses are considered industry standard for beer, although some companies are beginning to offer 22 ounce standard beers.

Also use these for many cocktails such as a Long Island Iced Tea.

Pilsner Glass

A pilsner glass is a smaller beer glass than a pint. These glasses are usually ten or twelve ounces. These glasses are also called "schooners" or "half pints" and are often used to provide a beer back to accompany a shot.

Collins/Chimney Glass

Collins glasses are used for drinks like a Tom Collins. These glasses are also frequently used for juice drinks live a Sea Breeze or a Screwdriver. Some bars also use these glasses for Bloody Marys and Long Islands.

Rocks Glass

Rocks glasses are used to serve a single shot served over ice. These glasses are also very useful for mixing larger shots such as a Red Headed Slut or a Lemondrop Shot.

Bucket or Double Rocks Glass

Buckets are a classic cocktail glass. The are used for many mixed drinks including Margaritas and Bloody Marys. Also used for double shots.

Coffee Glass

Coffee glasses are used for any manner of hot drink. They are made of tempered glass that won't crack when heated, so they can also contain flaming drinks. Heat with warm water and empty before filling with a cocktail.

Brandy Snifter

Brandy snifters are used for serving brandy and other cordials such as ouzo. These glasses can also be used to serve hot drinks if they are made from tempered glass. The large inside space allows aromas to be captured and enjoyed by the drinker.

Cocktail or Martini Glass

Cocktail glasses are the classic "martini glass". These glasses can be used to serve any drink "up". This includes any martini style drink such as a Cosmopolitan, but can also include strained drinks such as a margarita served up.

Cordial Glass

Cordial glasses are small capacity glasses that are used to serve cordial liquors. Cordials include port and sherry. The small portion size is traditional and these glasses only have a capacity of three ounces.

Daiquiri Glass

Daiquiri glasses are curvy deep cocktail glasses good for frozen drinks. This style is a traditional shape for may tropical drinks that are served blended. These include frozen margaritas, piña coladas, and of course daiquiris.

Margarita Glass

Margarita glasses are similar in appearance to a cocktail glass. However, these glasses are suitable to serve drinks that are strained, on the rocks or even blended. These are great for margaritas and daiquiris as well.

Wine Balloon

Balloons are a traditional wine glass that offers a large open air space above the surface of the wine. This air space allows for aromas to rise from the wine surface and be trapped to be savored. This is similar to the function of a brandy snifter.

White Wine Flute

Wine flutes are used to serve sparkling white wines. The smaller amount of surface area of the wine slows the heating of the wine. The downside is that you are able to experience the scents of the wine much less.

Tools of the Bartender

Just like a doctor or and electrician have special tools to carry on their craft, a bartender has a wide array of specialized tools to assemble drinks. This section will familiarize you with these tools and describe how they are used. The tools presented in this section should be considered standard issue for any bartender and should be present behind any bar that you will find yourself working in.

Shaker

A shaker looks like a steel pint glass. This tin is used to mix ice and ingredients and to shake them into a finished mix. These tins can also be used on speed mixers for making whipped cream and smoothies. Some are equipped with a straining lid.

Strainer

A strainer is used to drain the liquid portion of a cocktail out of a mixing tin without allowing ice to enter the drink. These are primarily used for making martini style drinks.

Zester

A zester is used to peel off a piece of citrus peel to garnish a drink. This peel contains a great amount of the oils of the fruit and can be used to flavor neutral liquors like vodka.

Jigger

1 oz / .5 oz

A jigger is the bartender's primary measuring tool. This tool is used to measure out one shot or one half shot depending on which side of the tool is used. When this tool is not in use, it should sit in a glass full of soda water. Soda water is a mild acid that will help keep the tool clean and ready for use.

Pour Spout

A pour spout is a tool similar to an oil can opener. This piece is inserted into the mouth of a bottle and is used to pour liquor quickly. Some units have mesh to block insects, automatic measures or even shot counters.

Rimmer

A rimmer provides the stickiness needed to get sugar or salt to stick to the glass. In essence it is nothing more than a sponge that is soaked in a juice. Roll the glass on the mat and then roll it in the sugar or salt.

Photo courtesy of www.BarProducts.com

Cocktail Spoon

A cocktail spoon is a simple long handled spoon. This tool is used to control the head on beer without waste, build layered drinks without mixing and to mix cocktails.

Photo courtesy of www.BarProducts.com

69

Juicer

Fresh squeezed juices make mixed drinks more flavorful and impress customers. As such, many bars are equipped with juicers. These are simple lever operated devices that can quickly squeeze a lot of juice.

Cork Screw/Bottle Opener

To open a bottle of wine or beer, you will need a corkscrew of some kind. These can be simple pocket versions that are kept on the bar or elaborate brass pieces that are fixed to the top of the bar for maximum speed.

Flash Mixer

A flash mixer is a specialized blender. A rotating blade on a long shaft is inserted into a mixing tin and engaged with a switch. These units can be used to mix whipped cream, quickly mix large batches of drinks, or blend a smoothie.

Muddler

A muddler looks like a small wooden club. This tool is used to crush ingredients that is placed in a mixing tin prior to making a cocktail. This operation is important for many popular drinks.

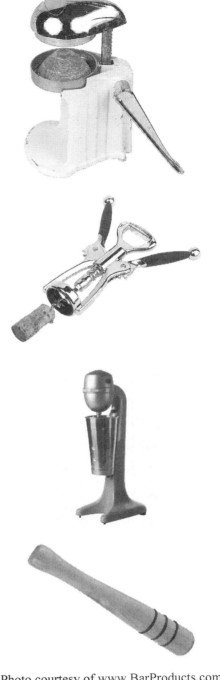

Photo courtesy of

Blender

Professional blenders are similar to the blenders you use at home. However, these machines are simpler to operate, only having a high and a low setting unlike a household unit. A quick flick of the switch is generally all you will need to blend any drink.

Necessary Terms & Definitions

Continuing with our comparison of bartenders to doctors and plumbers, bartenders also have specific jargon that they use to quickly communicate specific ideas and concepts while they are working. This "language" is not especially complicated and does not include a great many terms; however, you will need to know the following terms before you start work.

Liquor-A liquor is a mix of alcohol and other liquids including water, coloring, and flavoring.

Proof-the proof scale is a measure of alcohol in a liquor. This scale goes from 1 to 200 where "200 proof" is 100% alcohol. This means a liquor that is "80 proof" is 40% alcohol.

By Volume-"By Volume" is another means of measuring alcohol in a liquor. This scale goes from 1% to 100%. This means that a liquor claiming to be 26% alcohol by volume is 26% alcohol and 74% other stuff (includes water, coloring etc.).

Shot-A shot is a measure of liquor comprising 1.5 fluid ounces.

Build- Building a drink simply means mixing a drink in the glass it will be served in. All you do is add ingredients and stir.

Up- A drink that is served without any ice is called "up". This does not mean that it has not been shaken over ice.

Rocks- A drink served on the rocks is served over ice.

Neat- A drink that is served neat is served up, straight out of the bottle. This is common with high quality scotches and cognacs.

Double-Double the amount of alcohol. This does not necessarily mean double the amount of mixer. This makes for a much stiffer drink.

Muddle- Muddling means the crushing of ingredients in a glass with ice. This is accomplished with a muddler. It is common to muddle mint, citrus fruit or cherries.

Float-A float is a small amount of liquor that is poured on top of a mixed drink. This liquor is not mixed in but allowed to float.

Well or House- Every bar has a basic series of liquors that are used when a brand name liquor is not specified. These are called "well" or "house" liquors.

Premium-A premium liquor is any type of liquor that is not a well liquor and needs to be ordered by name.

Call-To "call" a liquor means to specify a premium liquor instead of a well or house liquor.

Sour-Sour refers to the mixer "sweet and sour". This often comes in a concentrate mix that is watered down and served. This can be mixed with vodka, melon liquors, amaretto or whiskey.

Collins- Collins mix is an equal parts mix of lemon and lime soda and sweet and sour mix. This is often mixed with gin, vodka or whiskey.

Press-A press mix is an equal parts mix of soda water and lemon and lime soda. A "press" is often mixed with whiskey or vodka.

Virgin or NA-Virgin means a non-alcoholic version of a cocktail. This often is requested for piña coladas, daiquris or margaritas. NA is another term for non-alcoholic. This phrase is often used in conjunction with beer.

Tall-"Tall" means extra mixer but the same amount of alcohol. This makes a larger beverage that takes longer to drink and slows the consumption of alcohol.

Twist-Asking for a "twist" is a means or ordering a slice of either a lemon or a lime with a cocktail. This is common with vodka and gin drinks.

86-86 is bar jargon meaning that an item is out of stock.

Shaken-Shaken means pouring the liquor and mixers of a cocktail into a shaker and shaking. You can then return the entire contents of the mixer to a glass, or strain the mix and serve the cocktail up.

Conclusion

Now that you have a basic understanding of the tools and terms that you will find behind the bar, along with the glasses you will be filling, you are ready to begin learning how to mix drinks. This will be covered in the next chapter.

Chapter 5 Review Questions

1. What type of glass would be appropriate for a scotch on the rocks?

2. What type of glass would be appropriate for a red wine?

3. Describe the process of sugar or salt rimming a glass? What else can be used instead of a rimming mat?

4. How many fluid ounces is a standard shot or jigger? In a half shot?

Answers

1. A rocks glass would be most appropriate but a bucket glass will also do.

2. A balloon would be the best type of glass. This will allow the aromas to collect in the glass and be enjoyed by sniffing.

3. Roll the rim of the glass on a rimming mat and then roll the rim of the glass in sugar or salt. Half of a citrus fruit also works in place of a rimming mat.

4. A standard shot is 1.5 fluid ounces. A half shot is .75 fluid ounces.

Chapter 5
Mixing Cocktails

Mixing cocktails is the most common, most complicated and most romantic aspect of working as a bartender. Learning this art (and it is an art) will take time and patience. You will need to be dedicated and study the recipes in the back of this book. Knowing your recipes well and being able to recall them at will is of enormous help when working as a bartender. With time, your skill at mixing drinks and knowledge of more obscure drinks will grow. Remember, when you learned to read you started slow and were not an expert overnight. Mixing cocktails will be no different.

Your bar should be equipped with all the tools that were discussed in the last chapter. As such, I will refer to these items throughout this chapter as I am discussing how to make cocktails. If you need a refresher as to what these tools are and what they are used for, please refer back to Chapter 5.

Mixers

Up to this point we have talked a great deal about liquors. However, cocktails are a mixture of both liquors and other ingredients called mixers. In this section you will find a brief description of the mixers that you will find in any bar. If the mixer (for example simple syrup) is something that you will need to make in the bar, a description of the process used to make it will also follow.

Simple Syrup – Simple syrup is a mixture of equal parts sugar and water dissolved into a solution. Essentially simple syrup is nothing more than sugar water. You can make this by adding hot water from a sink, or you can use a coffee maker as well. Both methods will produce water hot enough to dissolve the sugar. Once the water is added, stir the mix vigorously until no solid sugar remains. Allow to cool if you can. This solution is used in many cocktails to sweeten lemon and lime juice.

Cola – Cola is any soda flavored with the cola nut. This is a basic mixer. Cola is commonly mixed with whiskey and rum.

Lemon & Lime Soda – Many lemon & lime sodas are popular today. These are commonly mixed with vodkas and whiskey.

Tonic Water – Tonic water is water that contains quinine. Quinine is a bitter chemical that has anti-malaria properties. This fact made tonic water very popular in the tropics during the colonial period. Tonic is commonly mixed with gin or vodka.

Soda Water – Soda is simply water with carbon dioxide dissolved into it. This mixer is popular with vodka and whiskey.

Sweet & Sour – Sweet and sour is a popular mixer. This mixer has a sweet flavor followed by tartness. This mixer can often be made in house by adding sugar to lemon or lime juice. You can do this to order by muddling two sugar cubes with two ounces of citrus juice. Prepared mixes are also common. Follow the directions on the bottle. Mix this with vodka, melon liquors, and amaretto.

Juices – OJ, Cranberry, and Grapefruit – You may use other juices in the bar where you will work such as pineapple and pomegranate. However, these three are the main stand alone juices. It is not at all uncommon to receive orders for vodka mixed with any of these juices. Additionally, your bar should be equipped with lime and lemon juices. These are often used in shaken cocktails, but you will need to add simple syrup added to them before use.

Collins – Collins is a mixture of sweet and sour mixer (which can be sweetened lime juice) and lemon lime soda. These flavors blend nicely to make a crisp and refreshing mix that is very enjoyable on hot days. Collins mixers are served with vodka, gin and whiskey

Press – A press is simply a mixture of soda water and lemon & lime soda. This is a mixer that is commonly ordered with vodka or whiskey.

Ginger Ale – Ginger ale is a soda that is flavored with the ginger root. This gives it a tart, spicy flavor. This combination makes ginger ale a great mixer to blend with whiskey.

Energy Drinks – In recent years there has been an explosion in the beverage sector known as energy drinks. These drinks are very sugary tart beverages that have very high levels of caffeine. Many of these mixers exist and the market is still evolving with no clearly dominant brand. However, many bars choose to stock and serve at least one of these products. They are especially popular with younger drinkers who are looking for energy to continue drinking and a mixer to mask the flavor of the alcohol. Energy drinks are commonly served with vodka.

Cream – Half & half is the common cream product that is used as a mixer. This mixer is commonly blended with vodkas, coffee liqueurs and Irish creams to make a creamy, smooth finished cocktail.

Grenadine – Grenadine is not a mixer in the true sense of the word. No one will ever order a vodka & grenadine. Instead, grenadine is added to cocktails as a float in the finishing stages. It is commonly added to drinks such as a Tequila Sunrise and sometimes a Manhattan.

Dirty – Dirty is also not a mixer per se but is a way to request that olive juice be added to a cocktail. This is a common request with martinis. Adding olive juice will add a salty flavor that pairs well with gin or vodka.

Cocktail Mixing: The Basic Process

The process of making a cocktail is simple and can be broken down into several easy to remember steps. These steps are:

- Select and prepare the appropriate glass.
- Properly mix the cocktail using an appropriate recipe.
- Finish the cocktail and garnish it.

No matter what cocktail you are making, its construction can be broken down into these three steps. Once you have completed all of these steps, you will present the drink to the guest.

Each part of this chapter will discuss one of these steps in detail. I will discuss the many different procedures that you can carry out when completing one of these steps. You will not use all of these procedures on every cocktail. You will only use those that are appropriate to the drink you are making. All that being said; let's dive right in and get started.

Part I: Selecting and Preparing Your Glass

Selecting Your Glass

Some bars that you work in will have standard glasses that you are to use for each of the cocktails you make. These may be spelled out in a black and white manual three times as thick as this book. This will be the case in corporate owned chain restaurants. On the other hand, if you are working in a blue collar, family owned bar, the standards may be much more informal and are at the discretion of the bartender. In that case, use your best judgment. If someone orders a shot a tequila, it would not make any sense to serve the shot in a cocktail or Collins glass. It would make sense to serve the shot in a shot glass. Similarly a Long Island Iced Tea will not fit in a bucket or a rocks glass so those too would be a poor choice.

You can be flexible with your glass selection. There may be times when you are out of a particular glass type. A new dishwasher may drop your whole supply of cocktail glasses. If that happens, you can switch to a wine balloon. This may require some explaining to your guests. They will most often get a chuckle from the story and accept the cocktail. Along a similar line, a bucket and a Collins glass are similar (although not exactly the same) size. You can get away with using these glasses interchangeably as well. The rules of thumb are these:

- If the bar you are working for has spelled out their glass standards, follow these religiously.

- If the bar has loose or no standard glassware, use your best judgment and try to be consistent. See what other bartenders are using.

Making sure that your glass is clean seems like a simple thing. However, in the low light of a bar, or in the haste of a happy hour rush, this can be overlooked very easily. Nothing is more embarrassing than having a guest return a glass of wine to you because the lipstick print of the last user is still on the glass. This reflects poorly on you as a bartender, and poorly on the cleanliness of your bar. Avoid this problem by always using care in selecting a clean glass.

Chill Your Glass

Many cocktails are best served in a cold glass. For example, a martini will quickly absorb heat from a glass and lose the refreshing frostiness it gets when you shake it. As a rule of thumb, if the cocktail you are serving needs to be cold, but is served without ice, you must chill it. An example of this is a martini or a Manhattan served up.

You can always chill your glasses. This can be done in two different ways. The first technique is to store your glasses under refrigeration. This will ensure that they are always cold. Storing glasses under refrigerated conditions takes up a lot of space. Many bars will keep beer glasses in refrigerated storage but not glasses for cocktails. For all cocktail glasses, use the other technique.

The other technique is to place ice in the glass and fill it up with water. This will quickly pull the heat out of the glass and make a much more enjoyable drink. After about twenty seconds, dump the glass out and continue with making your cocktail.

Pre-heat Your Glass

If serving cold drinks in a cold glass is best, it makes sense that serving a hot drink in a warmed glass would be best as well. Cold glass will quickly suck the heat out of mixers like coffee, hot water, tea and hot chocolate and cool the drink. A cocktail that is only lukewarm when it should be hot is a big disappointment. Always preheat hot drink glasses.

To properly heat a glass, fill it with hot water. It is really nice to have a coffee maker behind the bar for this reason. Most of these machines have hot water spigots that can be accessed whenever hot water is needed. If you do not have a coffee maker, or it does not have a hot water spigot, it is best to fill up an insulated coffee pot with hot water for your use. Once you have filled the glass, again, allow it to sit and heat up. Once it is warm, dump out the hot water and proceed with mixing your drink.

Rimming Your Glass

Rimming a glass is the process of "sticking" a substance to the rim or lip of the glass. This can be anything. The most common substances that are used to rim a glass are salt and sugar. Along with sugar and salt, you can also use other substances like hot chocolate mix for Chocolate Martinis and a salt and pepper mix for Bloody Marys. Salt adds flavor to a Margarita and sugar sweetens up a Lemondrop. Also, a decorated rim adds to the appearance of a drink. If you are planning on using a salt rim, always use kosher salt. This type of salt is larger than iodized table salt and makes for a much better rim.

To actually get the sugar, salt, pepper, or hot chocolate to stick to the glass, you will need to roll the glass on something sticky. You can use a rimming mat that is soaked with sugar water or a piece of freshly sliced citrus fruit. Either one will work well. Take the glass and place the rim in contact with the rimming mat or the fruit. Gently press down to make sure a good amount of juice or sugar water is left on the glass. Next, just roll the rim of the glass in a bowl or tray that contains your salt or sugar. This will leave a nice rim of any substance on the glass.

A sugar or slat rim will add to the flavor or appearance of your cocktails.

Muddle Your Fruit or Mint

Some cocktails will require you to muddle solid ingredients in them before you add the liquid ingredients. Muddling is simply the process of crushing these solid ingredients before adding liquor and mixers. Crushing these items will extract juices and oils and make their flavors much stronger and enjoyable in the drink. Examples of items you will muddle include mint for Mojitos and Mint Juleps along with oranges and cherries for an Old Fashioned. Freshly muddled limes are great for Margaritas and fresh lemons make the best Lemondrops.

To muddle these ingredients you will need a muddler. Place the ingredients in the glass or mixing tin and add ice on top of them. Hold onto the glass with your left hand tightly. Then use the muddler in your right hand to crush the contents of the mixing tin. This action will crush the ingredients and also crush the ice.

Once the ingredients have been muddled, you can use the glass and its contents to build a cocktail or you can shake a cocktail with the contents and strain the resulting mix into a cocktail glass.

Fill The Glass With Ice

The last step in preparing your glass before you mix your cocktail is to fill the glass with ice. Ice is a bartender's best friend. You can never have enough ice in a glass, so fill the glass to the top. If you do not put in enough ice, the ice will melt quickly and water down the drink. Also, too little ice means that you will add to much mixer to the cocktail and make it weak. No guest will enjoy this. You can even add a little too much ice to the point where it is heaping out of the top of the glass.

Part II: Procedures For Mixing Drinks

Once your glass is prepared and ready to go as required by the drink recipe, you are ready to make your cocktail. This section is going to discuss the techniques that are used to make cocktails. You will be able to use one of the procedures outlined in this section to make any cocktail that a guest will order.

Liquor Pouring & Cost Control

Before we get started talking about mixing cocktails, we need to discuss techniques for actually pouring alcohol from a bottle into a cocktail.

Liquor is expensive and most bars that you work for will try to keep the amount of liquor that is poured into a cocktail to a minimum requirement. Any extra liquor that is added to a cocktail beyond the specified minimum is lost profit and added expense to the company. Most companies take these costs and lost profits very seriously. You can lose your job if you do not take cost control as seriously. Of course, some neighborhood bars are far less strict about this as well and will not even bother. Most will not.

In order to minimize lost profits and added costs, bars will often require you to measure the amount of liquor you are placing in a cocktail. There are two methods that are used to measure the amount of liquor that is placed in a cocktail. These are "jigger pouring" and a "free pour count". Some bars also have pour spouts that measure exactly one shot. In my experience these are not in common use. As such, I will not refer to them again.

Jigger pouring is the pouring of alcohol using a jigger as was described in the last chapter. The jigger will have two cups in most cases. One will be a full shot and the other will be a half shot. Which one you use will depend on the recipe for the cocktail you are making.

To use a jigger, hold it over the glass. This way, if you spill any liquor it will fall into the glass. This is shown in the picture on the next page. Fill the jigger all the way and when the measuring cup is full, stop pouring. Then tip the measuring cup so all of the liquor falls into the glass. Do not fill the jigger up and tip it while liquor continues to pour into the glass. This is called a "tail" and is wasted liquor and lost profits.

Pouring with a jigger takes a little practice. You will spill a little at first. To help with this, get a bottle, a jigger and a pour spout. Fill the bottle with water and just start pouring. A little practice this way will help you a lot in the long run.

When using a jigger fill it all the way over the glass. Quickly dump the liquor into the glass when it is full. This will help prevent spilling.

The other means of shot measurement is called a "free pour count". Free pouring is the process of pouring the liquor right from the bottle into the glass or mixing tin. There is no measuring device in this process. Instead, the bartender counts, in their head, while they are pouring the liquor. Generally, a "four count" is used for a shot and a "two count" for a half shot. Count quickly. There is no need to say "Mississippi" or "Hippopotamus" while you are counting. Simply count off "one, two, three, four" and stop.

You will not pour exactly one shot on a four count when you are beginning to free pour. You will need to develop and refine your sense of timing. This is also done with practice. Start free pouring and use your count. Pour off one shot, and then with a jigger, measure what you have poured. If it is too much, count faster. If there is too little liquor, count slower. After a little practice you will get the hang of things.

The Shot

A shot is the basic cocktail. All you have to do to make a shot is to pour the ingredients of the cocktail into a glass. There are a few different ways to pour a shot however. The difference lies in the glass that you select as the bartender.

A **straight shot** is one type of liquor poured into a shot glass. This is common with whiskeys, vodkas, and tequilas. You will not get many requests for shots of gin or rum. These liquors are much more commonly mixed in cocktails.

It will be very common for guests to request high end whiskeys such as single malt scotch and Irish whiskey **neat.** This means that they would like a single shot of whiskey in a glass. This is basically the same thing as a straight shot. However, you will need to use a rocks glass to serve the shot. When someone orders a neat shot, they are planning on sipping it. A rocks glass, instead of a shot glass will trap the aromas of the liquor better and provide a much more enjoyable sipping experience. Whenever someone orders a whiskey neat, ask them if they would like a few ice cubes in it. This is not the same thing as putting a shot on the rocks. If the say yes, add one or two cubes. Do not add any more than that. This adds just a touch of water to help unlock the flavor of the liquor.

Brandy, cognac and cordials are special cases of the shot. Shots of these liquors should always be served in a snifter. People drinking these styles of liquor will sniff them a lot. The snifter will help trap the aromas and allow the guest to savor them more easily.

Some guests enjoy brandy and cognacs heated. This is especially true on a cold winter day. The easiest way to heat a brandy snifter is to use very hot water and a bucket glass. With the hot water in the bucket, lay the snifter across the mouth of the bucket glass and allow it to sit in contact with the hot water. If the water is about to overflow, tip some out and reposition the glass. Be careful with the hot water. With the water in contact with the glass, the brandy will quickly hit up and become aromatic.

Layered Shots

You can also create shots that are layered. This happens when liquors will float on top of each other and not mix. This is a tricky process to do but can be learned with a little practice and patience.

The effect that is produced from a layered shot is really worth the time.

When pouring a layered shot, you will need to be careful to not mix the liquors. This is done when you break the surface tension of one of the liquors. Pouring straight from the bottle into the glass will always cause the layers to mix. To cushion the blow of the liquor coming out of the bottle, it is best to pour on the rounded side of a cocktail spoon. The liquor will run down the spoon and gently start pooling. This will allow you to float the liquors on each other.

A properly layered shot is a beautiful sight to see.

If you do not have a cocktail spoon you can tip the glass and pour along the angled side of the glass. This is similar to when you pour beer. You are shortening the distance the liquor needs to fall and cushioning the impact when it hits the other layers of liquor. This technique is less successful than the spoon technique but can work in a pinch.

Building A Drink

The shot is the simplest of all cocktails to make. After the shot, the next easiest technique is to build a drink. Built drinks are always served on ice, so you will need to fill whatever glass you are using with ice before you start.

To build a drink, add the necessary liquors to the glass and add the mixers. That's it. Once all the liquids are in the glass, mix the glass them up with a straw. Your drink is done.

There are many drinks that you will build. These include Margaritas, Screwdrivers, Greyhounds and White Russians along with many others.

Blended Drinks

Blended drinks are just about as easy to make as built drinks. The only difference is that you build the drink in a blender pitcher before you pour it into a glass. When building the drink in the pitcher, try to use the same amounts of ingredients that you would use in a regular built glass. You can even build the drink in a glass to measure properly. Then dump the whole mix in the blender. However, add about 20% more ice than you normally would. The volume will be reduced by the blending action. When you are all done blending, you should have a perfectly portioned cocktail.

When blending the cocktail, flick the switch of the blender on and off intermittently. Keep the motor on only for short bursts. This will make sure that you do not over blend the drink.

You can also make batches of drinks with the blender. Most commercial blender pitchers are at least two quarts in capacity. These can easily accommodate six large cocktails.

You can also use a blender as a cheat. Instead of having to make six mojitos in a row (a time consuming process) you can skip muddling the mint in the glass and let the blender do the work for you. This will save you a lot of time.

Shaken Cocktails

Many of the cocktails that you are going to be making as a bartender are going to be shaken. Shaking a cocktail is the process of mixing the drink with ice. This process produces a very cold drink without having ice in the glass. After mixing, the liquids are strained out and the cocktail is served up. Usually a martini glass is the glass of choice for any shaken cocktails. This is not always the case, however. Margaritas are also great after they have been shaken and served on ice.

To shake your cocktail, you are going to need a shaker. Fill the shaker about 60% full of ice. Then add your liquors and mixers. When all the ingredients are in the shaker, you are ready to shake it.

Home bars are generally equipped with a shaker like the one pictured in Chapter 4. They have a lid and a built in strainer. These are fine for the home bar. However, they are impractical in a busy bar. Lids and tops get lost and the built in strainer is too slow. Instead most bartenders will use the tin of the shaker and a pint glass.

I always use a plastic pint glass and you should too. Often times, you will need to bang the shaker/pint glass combo on the bar to get them to open. This can cause the pint glass to break. This is a safety hazard and a real inconvenience. Using a plastic pint glass eliminates this risk.

To shake the cocktail, turn the pint glass upside down and insert it into the mouth of the tin. Then shake vigorously. You should feel the steel can get noticeably colder. Shake at least ten times. When you are done, use a strainer to strain the cocktail into the glass as shown in the following picture.

Once you are done shaking the cocktail in the mixing tin, use the strainer to keep ice from falling into the finished drink.

Burning Drinks

Some drinks require that you light alcohol on fire before mixing the drinks. This is done both to provide heat to melt a sugared rim or to provide an effect to wow the guests. Either way, you will need to be careful. Alcohol is a fuel just like gasoline and burns very hotly. If you spill it you can start a fire or burn yourself. When I was first starting out I did both and this taught me a healthy respect for a burning glass.

The most common alcohol to burn is an overproof rum, although high proof whiskeys also burn easily. Commonly this style of rum is called 151 Rum. Many of these bottles even have a warning on them advising the user that the contents are dangerous.

Pour a little of this rum into a **tempered** glass. If the glass is not tempered, it may break from the heat of the fire. This is also dangerous and inconvenient. Once the liquid is in the glass, light it with a match or lighter. A long barbeque lighter works great too and offers a little more safety. It may flare so use caution. Never pour liquor from the bottle into a burning glass. This is a real danger.

If you are using the flame to caramelize a sugared rim (as with a Spanish Coffee), allow the flame to do its work. I often swirls the liquor around to get more of a flame. Don't rush it. When the rim is sufficiently caramelized, extinguish the flame with coffee or another mixer. Again, do not pour liquor into a burning glass. Continue building the drink until it is complete.

Part III: Finishing and Garnishing Your Cocktail

The last step in making a cocktail is the finishing and garnishing of the drink. This is the step where you make sure that the drink is attractive and pleasing to the eye of the guest. This step is no less important than the preparation and mixing steps. If the drinks you produce do not look good and instill a feeling of value in your guests, they will not buy more, may not return, or will tip you less than you deserve. Impressive looking, well made drinks will always bring in the crowds and the bucks.

Finishing Your Drink

Finishing a drink means adding a final ingredient to the cocktail. However, this ingredient is not intended to be mixed into the drink. Instead, this ingredient is added in a manner that enhances the drinks eye appeal. Once the guest has received the drink, then they will often mix it in as they deem fit.

Straws & Umbrellas

Any drink that is served on ice should have a straw in it. Many people's teeth are sensitive to cold and a straw prevents any pain. Before adding any whipped cream or liquor floats, add your straws. Placing the straws in the drink before these steps will ensure that the layering of the drink is not disturbed.

Cocktail umbrellas are also commonly added to tropical drinks. If the bar that you are working in makes use of cocktail umbrellas, add them before you garnish the drink, but after adding ingredients such as whipped cream and floats of liquor.

Whipped Cream

Whipped cream is appropriate to any cocktail that is made with coffee or hot chocolate. I have also seen whipped cream added to cocktails made with hot cider and hot teas. It is best to ask in these cases. When mixed into a cocktail, whipped cream adds a rich and creamy texture to any cocktail.

Many bars use aerosol whipped cream. This is an easy product to use and many of the people who will read this book will have used it many times. If the bar you work in uses whipped cream in this manner, simply point the nozzle of the can at the surface of your drink and apply some whipped cream. Aerosol whipped cream is mostly air so it will float on the liquid easily.

Many bars do not use aerosol whipped cream. Instead, these bars will whip heavy whipping cream behind the bar for that homemade taste. This is easy to do using a flash mixer.

To do so, fill a flash mixing tin about half way with heavy whipping cream. Next, add about a teaspoon of sugar and a few liberal dashes of vanilla extract. Then, place the tin on the mixer. Allow the contents to mix for a few minutes until the cream is thick and has an almost solid feel.

Using "homemade" whipped cream like this is a little harder than using aerosol whipped cream. This is due to the fact that homemade whipped cream is denser than aerosol whipped cream and will mix with coffee or hot chocolate if the whipped cream is not poured in gently. If you are gentle when pouring in the whipped cream, however, the cream will float right on top of the drink and make a very nice sight. If you need to, pour along the back of a spoon as for a layered shot.

Liquor Floats

Some cocktail recipes require that a layer of a particular liquor be floated on top of an already mixed cocktail. This practice is called a "float". This practice is common with tropical drinks. Examples would include floating orange brandy on a Cadillac Margarita, or 151 rum floated on a Mai Tai.

It is important to understand that this liquor is not to be mixed in. This layer will remain distinct and separate from the mixed portion of the cocktail. Again, this is very pleasing to the eye and adds to the appeal of the drink.

Garnishes

Garnishes are fruits or vegetables that are added to a cocktail to make it look more attractive and festive. Additionally, these fruits and vegetables often compliment the flavors of the cocktail. People love eating salty olives with a martini or celery with a Bloody Mary. I am going to briefly discuss the most common garnishes that you will encounter. Some of these garnishes will require preparation by you, the bartender. These preparation techniques will be discussed as well.

Citrus Fruits

Citrus fruits are the most common garnish that you will use as a bartender. This class of fruit includes lemons, limes, oranges, and grapefruits. Any bar that you will work in will stock these items and you as the bartender will be responsible for preparing them to be used as garnishes.

Citrus fruit garnishes are usually paired with the mixers in the cocktail. For example, a Screwdriver which is vodka and orange juice will be garnished with an orange. A Kamikaze, which is made with lime juice, will be garnished with a lime and a Greyhound that is made with grapefruit juice will be garnished with a slice of grapefruit.

As I have said, you as the bartender will be responsible for preparing citrus fruit garnishes for use in your bar. Preparing citrus fruit will mean cutting the fruits. There are two ways that you will cut citrus fruits. These are the "wheel cut" and the "wedge cut".

Wheel cut citrus fruit is when the whole fruit is sliced along the width of the fruit and a cut, in the shape of a wheel, is placed on the glass. A slit needs to be made in the fruit from the center of the slice to the edge of the fruit. This will allow the fruit to hang on the side of the glass as show in the picture on the next page.

You can also slice the fruit in half along its length before slicing it and adding slits to allow them to hang on the glass. This is called a "half wheel cut". This method is preferred by many bars as it allows the maximum number of garnishes to be made from one piece of fruit. This slicing style is also the most appropriate for large fruits like grapefruits. A wheel is too big and a wedge cut is heavy enough to tip over a glass, but a half wheel is just right.

Using the slit that you cut on a wheel cut citrus fruit will allow it to hang on the glass. This adds class and makes a drink look even more fancy.

A wedge cut is a way to slice larger and, by extension, juicier pieces of fruit. For example, anyone asking for a lime for a tequila shot would be best served to receive a lime wedge. This slice style also makes the best fruit slices for biting. Anyone ordering a Chocolate Cake shot should receive a wedge cut lemon.

To cut a fruit into wedges, slice the fruit in half down the length of the fruit. Then slice each half into four equal parts as shown in the diagram below. Again, you will need to slit each piece to hang on the glass.

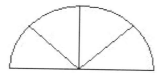

By slicing each half of a citrus fruit lengthwise in the manner shown in this image, you will produce juicy wedge cut citrus fruit garnishes.

Citrus Zest

Another way to use a citrus fruit as a garnish is to zest it. This is where you remove only the skin of citrus fruit and use the skin as the garnish. A citrus fruit contains many essential oils and can strongly flavor a drink made with neutral spirits like vodka.

To zest a citrus fruit, you will need a zester like the kind shown in Chapter 4. These tools have cutting edges that are used to gouge off the skin of a citrus fruit. Be careful, they can gouge your skin off just as quickly. This art can take a little practice to master. When you first start out, you will not doubt cut zests that are far too small. However, like most things in this book, you will improve with time to the point where your zests look like the ones shown below.

Olives

Olives are the traditional garnish of a martini. The salty flavor of an olive pairs very well with either a neutral spirit like vodka or a juniper bouquet from a Holland gin.

Olives are grown all over the Mediterranean coast and in California. Traditionally, olives have been stuffed with pimentos. Pimentos are type of red pepper. However, it is not uncommon to find gourmet stuffed olives that have many kinds of exotic and specialty stuffings. Specialty stuffings include jalapeno, bleu cheese, wild mushroom, almonds and even sardines. I would not recommend adding sardine stuffed olives to a martini without talking to your guest first.

The flavor of the olive compliments well with spirits in a martini.

Olives are used as a garnish by spearing them. This is where a thin piece of wood (often a long toothpick) is inserted through the olive. The spear/olive combination is then placed in the drink. Always make sure that the spear is above the level of the cocktail and can be lifted out by the guest. Nobody wants to fish an olive from a glass with their fingers.

Maraschino Cherries

Maraschino cherries are commonly paired with citrus fruit to add a color contrast to the garnish of a drink. The vivid colors of these cherries pairs very nicely with the green of a lime or an orange slice. Cherries are also added to virgin drinks such as a Shirley Temple. It has long been rumored that Maraschino cherries are made with formaldehyde, which causes cancer. This is absolutely not true. No formaldehyde is used in the manufacturing process. Even so, this urban myth continues to survive.

A cherry hung on the lip of a cocktail glass is far more attractive and practical than simply dropping it in the drink.

A decorative way to present a Maraschino cherry is to slit the cherry halfway. Then, just like a citrus fruit, the cherry can then hang on the side of the glass. This method is more decorative than just throwing the cherry in the cocktail.

Pickled Vegetables & Celery

Many bars stock a wide range of pickled vegetables. This category of garnishes commonly includes onions, beans, garlic cloves and asparagus. Pickled vegetables are often used in place of olives to garnish martinis. These vegetables will have a crisp tangy flavor and will come ready to use. No preparation is needed.

Another way that pickled vegetables are commonly used in the bar is to garnish Bloody Marys. Never be shy about garnishing a Bloody Mary. Use any type of pickled vegetable you have. Spear all the pickled vegetables together and place them in the drink. Guests will truly appreciate a good amount of garnishes. They also make the drink look great.

Celery is another great garnish to a Bloody Mary. To prepare celery for use, break off stalks from the bunch. Cut off any white parts of the celery at the bottom and shorten the stalks to about eight inches, but keep the leaves on the stalks. An example of what celery should look like in a cocktail is shown in the picture on the title page of this chapter.

Pineapple

Pineapple is a great garnish for any and all tropical drinks including Piña Coladas and any kind of Daiquiri.

It is important that pineapple garnishes be served with the fruit skin on. Otherwise, people will not be able to hold the fruit without getting sticky fingers. Canned pineapple is not made with the skin on the fruit. As a result of this fact, you will almost always need to prepare pineapple garnishes yourself using whole, fresh fruit.

Preparing a pineapple is not complicated. To start, remove the crown of the pineapple. Then slice the pineapple in half, lengthwise. Then, slice each of the two halves in half, again along the length of the fruit. The last step before slicing the quarters into finished garnishes is to core them. A pineapple is hard and inedible in the center of the fruit. Slice of the part of each quarter to the right of Line A in the diagram on the following page. This part is inedible. When that is done, cut each quarter into slices and slit them to hang on a glass.

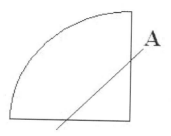

To remove the inedible core of a pineapple before slicing remove the portion to the right of the line marked "A".

Cinnamon

Cinnamon sticks add a real dash of class to any hot drink, especially those that have Irish cream and chocolate in them. There is no preparation required for these spices. These come dried in a jar and are immediately ready to use. If a drink has whip cream, a very nice trick is to float the cinnamon stick on the edge of the glass into the whipped cream.

If the bar you work in does not have cinnamon sticks, a dash of powdered cinnamon added to the whipped cream of a drink will add a nice flavor to the drink and a nice visual effect.

Cinnamon sticks like these add real class to any hot drink.

Learning Recipes

The first part of this chapter discussed much of the basic information that you need to start mixing cocktails. However, you still need to learn the basic drinks that you will be making in any bartending situation. In the Appendix of this book you will find most of the basic recipes you will need in any bartending situation. Of course people will come in and ask you to make something you have never heard of. If that happens, ask them what's in it and go from there. You can also buy a drink recipe guide. These books are many times as thick as this volume and contain more drinks than you could learn in a lifetime. Anytime you are stumped, you can always reference one of these as well. However, to start, focus on the ones listed in this book. They form what I call, "The Basic Drink Set".

At first, this seems like a very large and intimidating list of drinks that you will need to memorize. In fact most of these drinks are subtle variation on basic forms. If you can learn these basic forms, it is much easier to learn the Basic Drink Set. In the pages that follow, we are going to discuss five basic cocktail forms that cover 65 of the cocktails in the Appendix. With each form, I strongly recommend flipping to the Appendix and finding all the drinks that fall into this category. This will help reinforce the concept in your mind. Hopefully, when we are done, you will feel much more comfortable with these cocktails. You will still need practice but you will be on your way.

Basic Cocktail Form 1: Liquor &. Mixer

The easiest cocktail to make (other than a shot) is what I call "The Liquor and Mixer". This drink form is always served on the rocks in a bucket, Collins or pint glass. The basic recipe of this cocktail form is:

- One full shot of the primary liquor
- Mixer to fill the glass

It is really that simple. In fact, many of the drinks that fall into this category will have names that tell you the recipe. A perfect example is a "gin & tonic". Now that you understand the Liquor & Mixer Basic Form, you know that the recipe for a gin and tonic is one shot of gin and tonic water to fill the glass. This can be extended to many other drinks including "rum & colas", "vodka & orange juice" etc.

This basic form accounts for 27 drinks in the Appendix. You can find them by looking for the bold type that says "**Basic Form: Liquor & Mixer**". Many of the cocktails that fall into this category have fancy names like a Screwdriver or a Cape Cod, but they are nothing more than a single shot of liquor and one mixer to fill the glass.

Basic Cocktail Form 2: Double Liquor & Mixer

Adding one little step of complication to the first basic cocktail form will give you the second basic cocktail form. This is the "Double Liquor & Mixer". This basic recipe form is:

- One full shot of primary liquor
- One half shot of a secondary liquor

- Mixer to fill the glass

The only real difference between this cocktail form and the first form that was discussed is the addition of second half shot of liquor. Unlike the Liquor & Mixer Basic form, drinks of the Double Liquor & Mixer Form will not contain the recipe in their name. These cocktails will all be called by fun names like a "Pantydropper", "Hairy Navel", "White Russian", or a "Margarita". This basic cocktail form represents another 12 cocktails in the appendix. These are identified with the line "**Basic Form: Double Liquor & Mixer**".

Basic Cocktail Form 3: The Basic Martini

Not everyone knows that a traditional martini is another basic cocktail form. I like to call this one "The Basic Martini". The Basic Martini always contains:

- Two shots of the primary liquor
- A few drops of a secondary liquor

In addition to the basic recipe, martini drinks are always shaken in the process I have already described in this chapter. Martinis can be served either up in a cocktail glass or on the rocks depending on the preference of your guest.

This basic form only covers five drinks so I will cover them in more depth than the other basic forms. These drinks are also listed in the Appendix and can be found by looking for the line "**Basic Form: Basic Martini**".

Gin Martini – This is the classic martini. This cocktail is made with gin as the primary liquor and dry vermouth as the secondary liquor. Garnish with three olives or a citrus zest.

Vodka Martini – To make a vodka martini, simply use vodka as the primary liquor. You will still use dry vermouth as the secondary liquor. Garnish with three olives or citrus zest.

Gibson - A Gibson is a vodka or gin martini garnished with pearl onions. That is the only difference.

Manhattan – A Manhattan is a martini made with whiskey as the primary liquor and sweet vermouth as the secondary liquor. A Manhattan is garnished with a cherry.

Rob Roy – A Rob Roy is a Manhattan made with Scotch Whiskey. Everything else is the same, use sweet vermouth and a cherry.

Basic Cocktail Form 4: The Fancy Martini

The Fancy Martini is another basic cocktail form. This group contains 12 of the cocktails in the Appendix. To locate these drinks in the Appendix, look for the line "**Basic Form: Fancy Martini".** A Fancy Martini always contains:

- One shot of primary liquor
- One half shot of secondary liquor

Most fancy martinis will also contain one shot of juice and a shot of simple syrup. This makes these cocktails very sweet. They are very popular with drinkers who do not want to taste any alcohol. Sometimes, as in the case of the Apple Martini or the Chocolate Martini, no mixers is added and the liquors are served alone.

These cocktails are always shaken over ice in the manner described previously and are always served up in a cocktail glass. Garnishes will depend on the mixer that is used. For example, if you are making a Sidecar which is brandy, triple sec, orange juice and simple syrup, you will garnish the cocktail with an orange slice.

Basic Cocktail Form 5: The Long Island

The Long Island is the last basic form that I am going to discuss. This family contains another 9 drinks in the Appendix. These drinks are very commonly ordered in a bar and will make up a large part of your business. Knowing these drinks will be important so make sure you commit them to memory.

A member of this family is always built in a pint glass. The recipe will always contain the following:

- One half shot of vodka
- One half shot of rum
- One half shot of gin
- One half shot of another liquor
- First mixer to fill half the remaining space in the glass
- Second mixer to fill the glass

You will notice that rum, gin and vodka are ALWAYS present in a Long Island style drink. Remember this part and your work is half done. The only liquor that changes in these cocktails is the fourth. This will often be triple sec but can be many other types of liquor as well. Frequently, the first mixer will be sweet and sour or a juice. The second mixer will almost always be either lemon & lime soda or cola.

Conclusion

This chapter introduced you to the basic skill set that you will need to begin mixing cocktails. It may seem intimidating at first. It was to me. In reality, it is not very complicated and with a little practice and dedication, you will be able to join the ranks of successful and confident bartenders. Always remember that little acorns grow into mighty oaks. One day you can be that oak.

One step that I would strongly recommend taking, is to copy the Appendix of this book onto flash cards. Writing all of the recipes will help to commit them to memory and when you are done, you will have a set of flash cards to quiz yourself. This is what I did when I first started bartending and it helped me tremendously.

Review Questions

1. What is a whiskey press?
2. Describe the process of rimming a glass with salt.
3. How do you heat a brandy for a guest?
4. List three drinks that fit the Liquor & Mixer Basic Form.
5. List three cocktails that fit the Fancy Martini Basic Form.

Answers

1. A whiskey press is a cocktail of the Liquor & Mixer Basic Form. This cocktail consists of one shot of whiskey with a mix of soda and lemon & lime soda to fill the glass.

2. To put a rim on a glass, roll the lip of the glass (gently) on a rimming mat or piece of citrus fruit. Then roll the lip in a bowl of salt.

3. Brandy is best heated by laying the snifter in the mouth of a bucket filled with hot water. This will quickly heat the brandy.

4. There are many answers to this question. A Screwdriver, a Greyhound and a Gin & Tonic would all be acceptable answers.

5. Again, there are many answers to this question. An example answer would be a Sidecar, Lemondrop and a Kamikaze.

Chapter 6
Customer Service

The subject of customer service is the most important subject in this book. The tone of this chapter may seem fairly preachy. I am a true believer in this and some people think that my dedication to serving my customers borders on the fanatic. However, there is no getting around the simple fact that, without the continued and enthusiastic visits of our guests and their continuing flow of tips, none of us could have a career in bartending. At that point, we would all have to get a job in a cubicle somewhere. No thank you.

This chapter has many examples in it that illustrate the point I am trying to make in a clearer manner. These situations mostly deal with bartop or table service. In a walk up bartending situation, you will not have many problems that need resolving, you hand the guest the drink and the transaction is over when they have paid. However, always passionately take care of your guests. Never forget they pay your bills.

They Are Not Customers, They Are Valued Guests

In the introductory paragraph, I used the word "customer" to describe people that visit a restaurant or bar. I really hate using that word. I prefer to use the word "guest" as I have throughout this book. It is really a good idea to think of your customers as guests. This drives home the idea that the people that walk into the establishments we work in are not merely random people coming in to get food and drinks. Instead, it fosters the idea that these people are valuable and are more like family coming for a visit. This often creates a warmer, friendlier environment that is perceptible to the guests and encourages them to return for another visit. Bars and restaurants that take this philosophy seriously will often have regular visitors that show up every week, bring friends and family from out of town to the bar and use the bar or restaurant for special occasions like bachelorette parties and wedding receptions.

This idea can easily be extended to any interaction that you have with a guest. It encourages the mentality of caring about someone whenever you interact with them. This can be simple. It can include leading a guest to the bathroom instead of simply just pointing it out to them.

Once when I was on vacation in Europe, I arrived at my hotel in the middle of the night. I had been flying so long that I was exhausted and really needed to sleep. I was also starving. I had not had a chance to buy food at airports in between flights and there was no food served on the planes. I explained my problems to the front desk attendant. She explained to me that everything was closed in the area. She paused for a moment and then told me, while the restaurant was closed, she would happily make me a cold sandwich to take to my room. This was a godsend. I gratefully accepted her offer and left her a giant tip.

This woman was an inspiration to me and a credit to the service industry. She went out of her way to help me because she actually cared. This is a lesson that you should pay attention to and always try to mimic when you are behind the bar. I will never forget her for her help.

You should never miss an opportunity to help a guest in any way you can, as long as you comply with the law. If a regular ends up knocking on your door when you are closed and explains to you his son just flew back from a war zone and they want to have a drink, open the door and help them out to the best of your ability, as long as it is legal to serve alcohol. They will never forget you for that and they will always look at your bar fondly.

All that being said I will no longer use the term "customer" in this book. From now on, I will only use the term "guest".

The Guest Is Always Right...Even When They Aren't

It is simple, the guest is always right. They are right even when they are wrong. Accept it. There are exceptions to this of course but they are few. An example would be when it is clear to you that a guest is trying to cheat you and your bar.

If a customer tells you their food is cold, it is. If they say their steak is over cooked, it is. Accept what they say as serious and do your best to fix the problem. Never take a guests complaint personally. Most guests simply want their problem to be taken seriously and they just want your help in fixing it.

Never question or argue with a customer. There is nothing more cancerous to a guest's relationship with a restaurant as arguing with them. Take what they say as genuine and accept that they believe it to be important enough to be worth mentioning to you.

It Is Your job To Be In A Hurry

Hustle is a very important word in a restaurant or bar. Anyone who has ever worked in one of these establishments knows what I mean. Guests are always in a hurry. They want their food and drinks fast. They are often on a brief lunch break, have somewhere to be, have a plane to catch or are just plain hungry. It is your job to get whatever they want to them in a hurry and in just the way that they ordered it.

This can be hard. At the bar, you can often have many customers competing for your attention. If you are waiting on the tables, they can all sit down at once or they can ask for their check simultaneously. You may have food or drinks that they all ordered be done at the same time. Which do you take out first? Well, in reality, what you need to do is prioritize and try and get everyone's things out as fast as you can while forcing someone to wait a minimum of the time.

Look busy while you are doing anything. The worst perception you can give a guest is that their needs are not important and you have something better to be doing, or that you simply do not care. If you are moving fast and you look busy, many people will be very understanding and appreciate your hard work. If your guests see you standing around or chatting with your friends while they are in need of something, they will be less forgiving.

Never Be Afraid To Ask For Help

There are going to be times when you will be swamped with guests to help and a million things you need to do in order tohelp them. This is definitely a fact of life in the bar and restaurant business.

You should never be afraid to ask for help when one of these moments arrives. It does not mean that you are a bad bartender. What it does mean is that you are smart enough to realize when you are in trouble.

The flip side is also true, always be willing to help your coworkers out when they get in trouble too. With this kind of an attitude, working efficiently as a team is a simple extension.

Be Patient With Your Guests

Some guests can be very difficult at times and you must have patience. No matter what your interaction with a guest involves you must never loose control of your temper. You must always be in control.

Guests will ignore you. You may come up to a group that is talking or a person on their cell phone and try to take their order. They may simply pretend that you are not there. It can be frustrating. If you are serving multiple groups of people there is a rhythm to when you must visit each table and you will often only have a few minutes to help a table before another will need your help. A customer ignoring you or talking on their phone when you are trying to take their order will throw everything off. Be patient and keep an eye on them. Wait until they are off their phone or there is a break in the conversation before you return. In many cases they will appreciate your understanding and your patience.

Guests may acknowledge you when you come up to them, but then also ignore what you say. It is very common to tell a guest about the soup and any specials when they sit down. They will often ask you to repeat yourself. I always answer with a smile and happily repeat myself. They are there to have a good time and it is right that they are more focused on their dining companions than they are on you.

Guests will be rude to you. They will cut you off when you are talking and tell you they have been waiting for their food for an hour when you know it has only been twenty minutes. Get used to this fact right now. This can be hard. However, again, be patient and work with them. Be understanding and let any rudeness slide. Don't take it personally and remain professional. There are many reasons that this may be happening. They may have just broken up with their significant other. They may have just been fired. They may just have low blood sugar. Many times a cranky customer will become much friendlier once they are actually eating their food and having a drink.

Be A Good Listener

A little while ago, I was having lunch in a restaurant with a former coworker who had left the hospitality industry. We were having a conversation and suddenly we both just started laughing. The couple at the table behind us was having an argument about whose dog it was that was constantly relieving itself on their lawn. The woman was relating about she had slipped getting the newspaper that morning. Both of us had been listening to their conversation at the same time we were carrying on our own. We weren't even eavesdropping on a conscious level. We had simply both gotten so used to serving tables and listening in on our guests to know if they needed anything, that it was just habit. We couldn't even turn it off when we were not working. It was that ingrained.

This story illustrates a point. Always be listening. When your guests are ordering, listen to what they say and make sure you get their order right. When you are walking past a table or the bar, listen to what they are saying to each other. Did they say their steak was overcooked? If they did, ask how their steak is. They will tell you and appreciate you fixing the problem. You should even listen to the sounds of the restaurant. Anyone who has worked in a bar knows exactly what the sound of a breaking glass is. When they hear that sound, they know that there is broken glass somewhere that needs to be cleaned up and will grab a broom and dustpan.

When working in the bar, always keep your ears open.

Be Friendly

The most important advice that I could impart to anyone wanting to be a bartender is to be friendly. You should always be happy to see a guest walk in to your bar. It may be two minutes until closing, but you should still offer the same friendly service that a guest would receive ten minutes after you open. Remember that these people pay your bills with their tips. You want them to feel welcome.

Another reason to be friendly is that it makes customers like you. You can make a lot of mistakes in the service industry and be forgiven provided you are friendly. Never forget that for one minute.

Be Real

Many chain bars will force you to follow a set script when first addressing your guests. You will often have to tell them about specials, soups, and house specialty drinks. You may have to suggest some specific beverages. I have never really been a fan of this philosophy. I believe that if a bar is staffed with qualified, professional service employees, their authentic care for a guest's experience will always shine through. Also, it will be unscripted real concern rather than concern as dictated by an executive in a large corporate management office. Of course well established service standards are extremely important. However, this genuine sincerity is appreciated by your guests and helps to create a warm friendly environment to which they will return again and again.

Be Accommodating

You should always do your very best to give your guests what they want. This can mean many things. Often times, they will simply want you to add a special ingredient to their drink. It does not mean that you will not charge for the ingredient. If your bar serves food and a guest is on a diet or has a dietary restriction, it can mean they want you to serve a burger without a bun or they will want you to check and see if an ingredient is in a dish. This is common with allergies such as peanuts, wheat or gluten. Perhaps they will see if you can make them something that is no longer on the menu. If you can do it, you should always do it.

One common occurrence in a bar environment is someone on their 21st birthday, who has just received a drink recipe guide as a gift, to go through and ask you to make all kinds of bizarre exotic drinks no one has ever heard of. Help them make their special night worth remembering by mixing up whatever they ask for with a smile.

Sometimes, all that is required to be accommodating is to be do what you are supposed to do. Many bar people like to close up a few minutes early. If guest comes in a few minutes before closing time, they are often told the bar is closed. I have never been a believer in this. As I stated earlier, I will happily help folks out even after closing time as long as I am in compliance with the law.

Many bar and restaurant employees do not like when guests walk a few minutes before closing. They look at it as an inconvenience. They may have somewhere to be or they may just not feel like working any more. They may give substandard service or tell the guest that the bar is closed. This can be a big mistake. You never know if you might be chasing out a new regular or a big tipper. That guest may feel unappreciated and never return. Always give 100% service 100% of the time. Over the years I have gotten many large tips from appreciative late night guests when I have welcomed them in a few minutes before or after closing.

A common special need that a guest will bring to your attention will be a special dietary concern. This could mean that they are a vegetarian (no meat), vegan (no animal products at all) or could have a food allergy. One common allergy that comes up a lot is an allergy to gluten. Gluten is present in just about any grain or flour and flour is hidden in a lot of foods. You might need to read the ingredients on a package or ask your chef. Always go the extra mile to clarify and understand your guest's needs and do your best to help satisfy them. Don't be afraid to offer suggestions and help guide them to a proper choice.

The basic theme here is, that if you can do it for a guest, you should do it. A good saying to keep in mind is "The answer is yes. What is the question?"

Understand What Your Guest Wants And Give It To Them

Walk into any bar in the world and look around. You will see many different people, who want many different things. They all have different agendas. A person tucked away in the quietest part of the bar with a book, just wants to read and not be disturbed. Likewise, a couple having an intimate conversation may be breaking up and likewise wants to be left alone.

Businessmen from out of town, who are loud and have had a few drinks, generally want a good show and lively talk from the barkeep. They may want to know where they can meet local women and go dancing. They may also want to know where the closest "gentleman's club" is and how they can get there. They will appreciate your expertise and advice.

Some people will want you to talk their ear off and will not let you get away to serve your other guests. Some will just want standard issue quick and efficient service.

Your goal as a new service professional is to find out what each guest wants, of course without asking them, and give it to them. It is like a poker game, if you know what they want before they have to tell you, they will be surprised and impressed, will tip well and come back.

Guest Perception Is Everything

I have made references to this idea before this section. If a guest says that their food is cold, or their drink is wrong, it is. No ifs, ands, or buts. This applies to anything else that a guest perceives. If they believe a kitchen is unsanitary, they will not eat there and will tell all their friends about this perception. If they believe the service was slow or they were ignored, that is a true statement and it is your job to fix the problem.

Controlling a guest's perception and presenting your work and your establishment to them in a favorable light is an extremely important concern that you must have and a skill that you must develop if you are to be successful in your career as a bartender. Pulling a drink from someone who is intoxicated is much easier if you present your action as a helping, caring friend, rather than a stern disapproving parent. If you are friendly and helpful the guest will return and remember you fondly; if you are condescending, they will not.

There are many different ways that you can control what a guest perceives and it can change from guest to guest. A middle aged couple that is in for a quiet nightcap will not take kindly to profanity. However, when someone asks you what the letters in the name of the drink "A.M.F." mean, they often already know, and want to hear you say "Adios Mother Fucker!" They love it!

It can be as simple as the words you choose to use. How you talk to your guests is another way to control what your guests think of you and your establishment. Choose your words carefully and use them to maximum effect. For example, if you are out of coffee or it is old and you need a few minutes to brew a pot, try telling your guest this line "I don't have a lot of faith in this pot of coffee, can I talk you into waiting a few minutes while I brew a fresh pot?" The customer will now look at you as someone who is protecting their interests and making sure they receive a quality product. Whether it is true or not, they also believe that you are being honest with them and will frequently respect this trait as well.

The philosophy of controlling a guests perception and making sure that it is positive at all times, can be applied to absolutely every aspect of your service, person and demeanor while you are at work. Always keep it in the back of your mind.

Mistakes Happen

Things will go wrong in a bar or restaurant. This is a fact of life. Murphy's Law says if it can go wrong, it will. Get used to this fact and deal with it. Food gets dropped, burned or you will forget to order it altogether. You will make a Lemondrop with licorice liquor and you will get recipes wrong. I have just finished making a perfect coffee cocktail many times only to grab the pot of hot water and fill up the cup before I know what is happening. At that point, the whole drink will need to be remade. It's that simple.

How you deal with problems like this is what separates the men from the boys. The worst thing you can do is hide form your mistake and disappear. As a service professional, it is your duty to keep your guests informed as to the goings on with their order, whether it be food or drinks, good or bad. They may have theater tickets and need to be at the show in less than an hour. You don't know what their situation is, so you need to talk to them right away when a problem arises.

Honesty is good for any situation that a customer can understand. If there is a kitchen fire, or an employee has just been seriously injured, they can understand this and will be sympathetic to an honest straight forward approach.

Lying can also be ok. Make sure you do it in a sincere and honest tone. If something has happened that is harder for a guest to understand it can often make things easier if you explain it in simpler terms. For example, you are serving a table of ten people. The food is ready except for the well done steak, which for some reason has not even been started. This is a problem. The nine items that are ready will grow old and cold in the window waiting the 15-20 minutes for the well done steak. You have to take the food out, but you will also need to explain why you are missing that steak. This can be hard. I have always like telling them that I dropped the item. This makes me look like an idiot. Who would admit to that if it was not true? Often times the guest will laugh out loud, at your expense. However, the laugh generally softens the blow and makes them a little more relaxed. At that point the guest can decide what to do. You have given them the option. They may want to switch their order to a quicker item. You may need to give them the steak for free. However, the rest of the table is happy and the guest knows what is going on and will often be more patient in waiting for their food.

Find The Problem And Fix It If You Can

No matter what goes wrong in a service scenario, and no matter how you explain a situation to a guest, the bottom line is that it is your job to identify the problem and fix it...fast. This can be hard, and sometimes you will not be able to make everyone happy. Some will leave angry. There is not a lot you can do when a bride does not have her ID at her wedding reception and wants a drink. You cannot break the law. She will probably leave a little upset, but if you can fix it, do it. Enough said.

Conclusion

This chapter is only a few personal thoughts on the subject of customer service. This subject could easily fill several books of this size. The bottom line is to take care of your guests like you would your family (or anyone else you actually like). Make sure that they have a great experience, tell their friends and come back for another visit. If you take care of your guests, the rest of the pieces will fall into place with time, experience and hard work.

Homework Assignment #1 – Go To A Bar (Fun, Huh?)

If you are studying to be a nurse you will go to a hospital and observe. The same can be said police officer. Well it is no different with a bartender. You should go out to a bar for a visit. You do not need to tell anyone that you are coming or make any special arrangements. A bar is a public place and you can just take a table. Do it during a busy period so you can see the staff in action. Take a book, newspaper or laptop with you so you do not seem to be staring.

What I want you to do is watch the flow of the bar. See how the bartender conducts themselves. Watch how they make the drinks and what types of drinks they are making. See if they are working the bar alone and taking care of the tables as well as the bar. In short, take it all in and observe how they work. Ask yourself:

- What kind of bar environment is this?

- Is this somewhere I would like to work? If not, why? What kind of environment would you like to work in?

- What kind of uniform is required?

- Does the staff seem to be enjoying themselves and do they care for their guests?

Order a drink and a meal an spend and hour or so doing this. If cash is tight, try going during happy hour if cheap appetizers are offered. Consider this a work study program, but make sure to have fun. Also, there is no reason that you cannot repeat this homework assignment many times with different bars. The more knowledge you have of the bars in your area and the more exposure to them you can get, the better off you will be.

Chapter 7
Working In The Bar

Up until this point in the book we have discussed what you will be pouring and how you will be pouring it. This is core information that you will need in order to be successful as a bartender. However, beyond this information, you will need to know what to expect when you are working behind the bar. This chapter is going to provide you with just such information.

In this chapter we are going to discuss professionalism and preparing for work, the mechanics of serving your guests, tips, controlling your environment and how to mesh well with your coworkers to create a fun and profitable behind the bar experience.

Preparing For Your Shift

In order to set yourself up for success on a bar shift, you need to do a good deal of preparation. What follows are descriptions of the steps that I use before I show up for work and when I first get there.

I have always liked to think of a busy bar like one of those machine gun nests in a war movie. Running out of supplies is like running out of bullets. That is never good. You can help ensure that that never happens by following these steps once you begin working behind the bar.

Your Uniform

In many cases you uniform is the first impression a guest will have of you and your professionalism as a bartender. It is extremely important that this sends the right message.

Often, your uniform will be dictated by the restaurant or bar that you work in. Your employer will present you with this dress code when you first get hired. I cannot stress how important it is to follow this dress code. Do it even if you do not care for the uniform. No one wants to or needs to go looking for another job simply because one of their shirts had a barbeque sauce stain on the cuff.

Always make sure that your clothes are freshly washed and are in good condition. Before you put on a shirt, look at it. Does it look like you just pulled it out of a mayonnaise jar? If it does, iron it. If you do not have an iron or are pressed for time, and the clothing item is made of cotton, you can always throw it in the dryer on low for a few minutes to get rid of wrinkles.

Many bars will require their bartenders to wear a tie. If, you are issued a specific, company approved tie, ask for two. These will get dirty quickly and a backup is very handy. If you are allowed to select your own ties, make sure the tie is appropriate. However, you can have a lot of fun with this. I love to wear silly (but appropriate) ties on special occasions like Christmas and New Years. One trick with a tie is to tuck it into either your shirt near your stomach if your apron covers your chest. This will help keep the tie in place and will prevent it from falling into drinks. A synthetic tie meeting a flaming drink is not a good thing so always take this caution. If your apron does not cover your chest, you can also tuck your tie into your pants.

An apron is another essential part of a bartender's uniform. The style of the apron will also probably be dictated by your employer. If the apron style is not dictated by you employer, visit a uniform store and buy a supply of ten aprons in a style you like. These get dirty even faster than your ties so a large supply is a really nice thing to have.

There are three common styles of aprons. These are short aprons where the apron hangs to the mid-thigh. After that there is a knee length apron. This is my personal favorite. Lastly, there is the bistro apron. This apron style hangs near the bartender's feet. I do not care for this style as I always feel that I am about to trip.

Shoes are another very important part of a bartender's uniform. Where bartender's work, it is almost always slippery and wet. This creates a real safety hazard if you are not wearing the right footwear. It is really no fun slipping behind the bar and throwing a glass of red wine on a guest. Believe me!

To help with this, you need to make sure that you are wearing rubber soled shoes that are non-slip. Never under any circumstances wear shoes that have leather soles. These look nice but will feel like you are working on ice. For the ultimate in safety footwear, you can visit the website of an industrial shoe supplier. These companies specialize in providing footwear that will stand up to the needs of workers. These companies can provide shoe styles that are appropriate to any work situation from a steel mill to a fine dining French bistro.

The last three pieces of your uniform as a bartender are pens, paper and a corkscrew. You can never have enough pens. You may not write down orders in a bar, but guests will certainly want to pay you with a credit card. How will they sign these if you do not have enough pens? I always have <u>at least</u> ten pens on me when I show up for a bartending shift. Paper is needed to write down orders. Depending on the type of bartending that you are doing, you may need to take people's dinner orders. If this is the case and you have to get three groups worth of orders all in one pass, it is very helpful to have something to write it on. I like to use a check presenter with a bunch of ticket book pages stuck in it. It is also common to use ticket books or little spiral notebooks as well. There is no right answer to this one. Do whatever is most natural to you.

A wine key is also a necessity for the bartender. If a customer orders a bottle of wine while they are sitting at the bar, they will expect you to open it in the manner that was described in Chapter 3. If you do not have a wine key, this will be impossible. Trust me when I say it is a real pain to have to go look for a wine key while your guest is waiting for the wine they ordered.

Showing Up Early

Any shift that I work, I always show up a full half hour before I need to be there. This is a habit that took me a long time to develop, but I cannot stress its importance enough! There are three reasons that this is a great idea.

Firstly, if you already plan on showing up for your shift a full half hour early, then you have a built in time cushion in the event that you hit slow traffic or leave a few minutes late. Charlie Chaplin once said that a big part of life was just showing up. This is true. If you are always early, how can you be fired for being late?

Secondly, showing up early says to your employer that you are a good employee who takes their job seriously. A person like this is a real asset to a restaurant or bar manager and they will work to protect that asset. Also, they will often take this demonstration of professionalism into consideration when good shifts become available. It is just good business on your part.

Lastly, I like to show up early for a shift to get the lay of the land in the bar. I want to see if the bar is in a good state. Did the night bartender have a chance to get everything clean before they left? Did the day bartender have a chance to get all their stocking and preparation work done? If they did not and I am there a full half hour early, I can always help catch up. A little effort like this can often go a long way in making sure that your shift runs much smoother. One warning I will give you in this regard is never clock in early without talking to your manager first. If your reasons are valid and you want to help the business by making sure everything is ready, no decent manager will have any problem with your request. If you clock in early without permission, you may get in trouble.

Stocking Your Bar

Once you are behind the bar you will need to get it ready to go. If you are the day bartender, you will need to make sure that everything was done as it should have been the night before. If you are the night bartender, you will often be replacing the day bartender. Never let them leave until the bar is ready to go and you are ready to work. Don't take their word that everything is done. Check it yourself.

The first thing I always do when I get behind the bar is to look at everything. I see what I need more of, I look and find what we are out of and I look at the organization of the bar.

I love making lists. This helps me to remember what needs to be done. Odd as it may seem, I am a forgetful person and if I do not write something down, I will forget it. When I am looking around the bar, I am almost always writing down what I need and what needs to be done on a list. That way I know the current state of things and I know what still needs to be done. I strongly recommend when you first start working in the bar that you take full advantage of lists. You already have the tools you need as part of your uniform and it will make you more efficient and organized.

Liquor is the number one thing that you will run out of in the bar. You will pour a lot of it, but because it is an expensive item for a business to stock, it is often locked up. The process for stocking liquor will vary depending on your company's policies. It may be that managers will need to get the liquor from a lockup that only they can access, you may not be able to get in there. If this is the case, make a list of what you need right away and get it to the manager. They are often very busy people, so the sooner you get them this information, the better is the chance that they will get you the liquor you are low on before you run out.

If, on the other hand you, as the bartender, have access to the liquor lockup, go and get what you need and place them in the correct the place in the bar. Ideally, when stocking liquor, you should have one if not many full bottles behind any bottle that is in the process of being used.

Make sure you have lots of ice. If you did not get that ice is important in previous chapters, ICE IS IMPORTANT. Without ice, you are not making any cocktails. So, make sure that any ice wells that you have are overflowing, not just full before you start.

The next thing I do is check my garnishes. How long have those olives been there? If you won't eat your garnishes, then replace them with fresh items.

Make sure that you have ample amounts of glasses. If for some reason, you are low on a particular type of glass, go and get more from the stockroom or inform your manager if necessary. Not too many guests enjoy getting a top shelf martini served to them in a wine glass because you did not bother to go and break out another case.

Mixers are essential to the mixing process so make sure that you have the necessary amounts of any mixers available. This should always include:

- Cola
- Lemon & Lime Soda
- Tonic
- Soda Water
- Orane Juice
- Cranberry Juice
- Lemon Juice
- Lime Juice
- Grapefruit Juice
- Grenadine
- Sweet & Sour Mix

With the juices, it is very important that you pay attention to their freshness. This is especially true if they are fresh squeezed juices. These have a shelf life of only a few days and will impart terrible flavors, if not make your guests sick, if they have started to mold. The best way to check the freshness of the juice is to check the date on it.

If there is no date on it, smell it. If there is any doubt about the juice's freshness, throw it away.

Check your salt and sugar supplies. If the day has been busy these two important substances may be low. Also, if the bartender has had a spill or was in a hurry and was slinging juices everywhere, these can be quite polluted. If they are, replace them with fresh supplies..

After you have checked your bar itself and made sure that you have plenty of liquor, move on to checking your beer and wine supplies. Wine is easy to check. Make sure you have the most amount of wine bottles that you have space for. Most bars will have a rack system of some kind. If you do, just make sure it is full.

Beer in the bottle is just as easy. Always make sure your coolers are full or you have as much beer under refrigeration as you have space for. Beer in the keg is a little trickier. You cannot add beer to a keg. The best you can do is check and see which beers are low in the keg. These are the beers that will blow first.

Often when beer is delivered, it is just thrown into your beer cooler. It is rare that you will find a delivery driver who will carefully place the beer exactly where you will need it most. They are busy and are keeping a schedule. One thing that I like to do when I come on is go into the beer cooler and make sure that each keg that is on tap has its replacement keg right next to it. This will help you save time when you are changing a keg. Trust me that kegs never blow when it is convenient. They will only blow when you are very busy. This step can easily save you a couple of minutes when changing the keg. This makes you a much more efficient bartender in the long run.

The last thing that I always check before I get started is what the restaurant or bar is out of. This sort of thing happens and you need to know what you are out of to be able to keep your guests properly informed and to reflect positively on your bar. Many restaurants will keep a list of these items. This is called an "86" list. Items on this list are said to be "86ed".

I do each of these steps that I have described each and every time that I show up for a shift. They make my shifts much smoother, which helps me keep my cool and serve my guests better. This translates into better tips in the long run as well.

Banks In The Bar

When you are working as a server, it is not uncommon to work out your own pocket. This is where you provide your own change and you take in cash payments for the restaurant and keep it until the end of the night. This is almost never the case when you work as a bartender. You will almost always be issued a bank by the bar.

Being issued a bank means that you are given a sum of money, that you are then responsible for, to make change for the bar's guests. This can be a big responsibility. At the end of the night you better be able to hand the house its money or face the consequences. This is also one of the reasons that a bartender must present himself as a trustworthy individual. Stealing in a restaurant is easiest in the bar. There is a lot of money at stake and your manager needs to believe that they can trust you.

The first thing that you need to do when you are issued a bank is to count it. This does not say that you do not trust your manager or the bar. Instead this acts as a check to make sure that everything is up and up. It could be the case that whoever used the bank last counted wrong. Maybe your manager forgot to include that last roll of quarters. Trust me, when it gets busy mistakes happen. You counting your bank assures that you are taking responsibility for the right amount of money and that everyone has done their job.

If there is a problem with your bank whether it is short or has too much money, let the manager know right away. This will again show that you are a trustworthy and responsible employee. Again, this only makes you more valuable to the bar in the long run and makes your job safer.

Beyond counting your bank, make sure that it is in good condition. A $500 bank that is made up of five $100 bills is useless. You need to make sure that there are lots of small bills and coin. If you are low on any of this change, ask your manager for more.

Get Organized

When you are working behind the bar you need to have things the way that you like them. To make sure that you work quickly and efficiently, you need to get organized. Make sure you know where everything is and you have quick and easy access to what you need.

When a doctor goes in to conduct a surgery, they lay out their tools in a convenient and logical manner. This same idea works for a bartender. I like to keep my mixing tins upside down on the bar with their plastic pint glasses sitting right on top of them. That way when I grab one of the stacks, I have all the pieces I need to start mixing a cocktail right away.

Pens are another example. I keep a good supply of pens in my pocket at all times, but I also keep a cup of them on the bar ready to hand to a guest or replenish my pocket stash right away.

How you organize your bar will ultimately be dictated by your personality, and your work style as well as your bar itself. You will need to put a little thought into this to make it right. When you are working pay attention to what you are doing, if you find that you are spending a lot of time walking back and forth across the bar for martini glasses, find a way to put them closer to you. This will eliminate a time waste and means that you can help more guests in the same amount of time and make more money in tips.

Keep Your Cool

I cannot stress how important it is to keep your cool while you are working as a bartender. Shifts will be stressful, customer will be rude if not profane, and servers will yell at you when you are buried with drink orders. If you cannot accept these facts and keep your cool then you may need to think about another profession.

Freaking out will only compound any problems that exist. If you a buried with drink tickets, the tickets will keep coming while you are hyperventilating. If a guest has just called you something profane, returning the favor will only compound the problem and lead to a fight. **Remember that freaking out never helps anything. Always stay cool.**

Serving Guests In The Bar

Tabs

In the bar, you will often be required to run tabs for your guests. This is where you keep a running bill for the guest which you will present to them at the end of their dining/drinking experience.

Unfortunately, not everyone who walks into a bar will be a responsible person to whom the bar should issue credit. People will step outside to smoke or visit the bathroom. Also, when alcohol is involved, people may forget that they have a bill that needs to be satisfied. To protect the bar and your tip, you will often need to take some kind of collateral to ensure that the person will return to pay their bill. In many bars a credit card is used. This is especially true if the bar has a computerized point of sale system.

If your bar is computerized, start a check for the guest in your system with the contents of their first round and run the card. This puts the card in the system and makes sure that the card will not be declined and is not a stolen or canceled card. Always hold onto the card while the tab is open. If you give the card back to the guest they may wander off and you will not receive a tip when they fail to sign their credit card slip. This represents a loss to you and can easily be avoided by hanging onto the card.

While the person is in the bar, keep their card somewhere safe. Believe me you have not seen an angry guest until you explain to them that you have lost their company credit card and they are going to have to explain to their boss where it went. Also, keep with the card a current copy of the bill. Each time they order more things, replace the old paper copy with the current one. This is a good habit to get into and will make for a quick cash out when the guest is finished.

If your bar does not have a computer system, a driver's license is the best collateral to take. Everyone in your bar should have identification on them so it will be no problem getting it. Like before, keep a current copy of the guest's bill with the license and update the bill each time something is ordered. At the end of their visit, the guest will have the option of presenting you with a credit card which you may run while they are present or they may also pay in cash. Either way, they will be there with you if there are any problems.

If you are ever left with a credit card or license at the end of the night, let you manager know and put it with a copy of the bill in a safe lost and found location. It is entirely possible that your guest actually forgot to pay their bill and will return the next day looking for their card. When they do, you can present them with the bill that needs to be paid. In most cases, the guest will be terribly embarrassed and the bill will be paid promptly. You may even get that tip after all.

Bartop Table Service Program

In many bars guests have the option of sitting at the bar. Guests sitting at the bar may order food and drinks just as if they were sitting at a table in the restaurant. To serve these guests properly you will need to understand the basic points of table service and be able to carry them out. In this section, we are going to discuss how to serve these guests.

Step 1 – The Greeting

Whenever someone sits down at your bar you will need to acknowledge them right away. This is an extremely important step as it sets the tone for the whole experience in the bar. Often guests will never have been in the bar before and will be unsure of what to do. It is your job to acknowledge them as quickly as possible. This reassures the guest and puts them at ease.

You will often be running around behind the bar and you may be busy helping another guest when they first sit down. As soon as possible, let them know you will be right with them. Once that is done, finish helping the first guest and get back to them quickly.

Step 2 – Menus and Drinks

Almost everyone who sits at a bar is going to want a drink of some kind. That being the case, as soon as you get back to the person, ask them if you can grab them a drink. They will almost always ask for something. If they say they are waiting for someone and want to wait, automatically put a glass of water in front of them and let them know that you will keep an eye on them and wait for their guests to arrive.

Not everyone who sits at a bar is going to be interested in food. Because of this, I always ask guests if they would like to see a menu. If they say yes, I provide them with all the menus the restaurant offers. In most cases this will be a standard menu and a fresh sheet or periodic specials menu. Also at this time, I will inform the guest of any daily soups that are being served.

Once you have gotten a drink order and asked about menus, go and make the drink. This will give the guest time to look at the menu, if they are planning on having food, and make their selection.

Step 3 – Drink Delivery & Food Order

Once you have made the drink that the guest ordered, take it to them. It should have taken you a minute or two to make the drink, and for most guests that will be enough time to decide on dinner. If they need a few minutes, come back.

When the guest has decided on dinner, take their order. When I take a food order, I will set silverware and any needed condiments in front of the guest right after I ring in the order. Also, if the guest is alone, I will always offer them a newspaper. Most people will happily take it. Always keep a few newspapers behind the bar for this reason. They will help keep guests busy and relaxed while they wait for their food.

Also, while the guest is waiting for their food, keep them informed of the progress. If you talk to the kitchen and they tell you the food is almost done, pass that info on to the guest. They will appreciate it.

Step 4 –Food Delivery & Check Back

When the kitchen has finished preparing the food for your guest, get it out to them as quickly as possible. Hot food should always be your first priority. Many of the foods that are served in a bar environment grow cold quickly. This is especially true of fried foods like French fires and chicken wings. No guest will appreciate cold food and it reflects poorly on you and your bar.

When you are delivering the food, make sure that the guest has everything that they need. This includes napkins, condiments and silverware. Also at this time it is a good idea to take a look at the guest's beverage. How full is it? If it is less than half full, offer them a refill. The guest may decline. If they do, I always make sure they have a glass of water in front of them. Before you walk away, always ask if there is anything else they need.

Once you have delivered the food, you will need to check back on the guest and make sure everything is prepared correctly. It is possible the steak they are eating is improperly cooked or there are onions on the burger when they asked for none. Perhaps they realized they needed something while they were eating that did not occur to them earlier. Try and do this check back within a few minutes. However, make sure that they have actually touched their food before you talk to them again. It is silly to ask how food is before they have taken their first bite.

Step 5 –Bussing, Refills & Dessert

When your guest has finished with their meal, take their plates away. Again, look at the level of their drink and if it is low, offer a refill. In addition, offer coffee and dessert. Always offer coffee and dessert. These additional products can add a healthy amount to the guest's bill and will consequently add to your tip. It will also make your boss happy.

You can also offer coffee cocktails or an after dinner cocktail to your guest. Brandy, cognac, scotch and cordial liqueurs are traditional after dinner drinks. Many guests will take you up on this offer and these products add even more to the bill than a normal dessert or coffee would.

If the guest declines all of these offers, grab their bill.

Step 6 – Payment

When the guest has finished with their dining experience, you will need to present them with a bill. Always get the bill as quickly as you can. Keeping a guest waiting to pay is a sure fire way to lower your tip.

Once you have the bill, present it to the guest and inform them of how they can pay. In most cases, you will simply say something like "I will take care of that when you are ready". Leave the guest with the bill. They do not want you hovering over them while they figure out which card they are going to pay with or while they are getting cash out of their wallet. It is just like when using an ATM, privacy is appreciated.

Keep an eye on them, however. As soon as a form of payment (either cash or card) is out, make your way back to them and process the payment quickly. If you are running a card always make sure you present your guest with a working pen to sign the slip.

If you take in cash as payment, never assume the change is a tip. Always tell the guest you will be right back with their change. They may correct you and tell you that the change is yours. They may not. If they do not, always make sure that they have plenty of small change to leave a tip. Never give back all $20's. Also, put the bill on top that you would like to receive as a tip. Be reasonable, however. If the bill was $25 don't put a $20 bill on top. Twenty percent is a good tip, so in the case of a $20 tab, a $5 bill would be the best selection. Most of the time this will work and that bill will be left behind, if you did a good job that is.

Working The Bartop

It will often be the case that you have more than one guest or group of guests on the bartop. To work efficiently, you are going to need to learn how to serve all of these guests simultaneously. To anyone new to the world of serving, this can be a daunting task.

The best way to handle this situation it to use a medical concept called triage. Triage is the process of deciding which patient is in the most need of immediate help and which patients can wait. An example will help to illustrate this idea.

Imagine that you are a bartender in charge of a bartop that is currently seated with three guests. For the purposes of this example, we will call them Guest A, Guest B and Guest C.

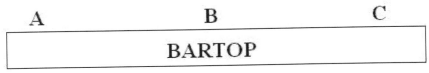

Example bartop.

Guest A has just sat down. There are no menus sitting at the bar. Guest B has a drink in front of them. When you dropped of the drink they asked for a minute to look over the menu. Guest C is currently eating a meal that they ordered. You have not checked to see if everything is alright, however, they are eating their meal and reading their newspaper.

Given the information listed above, which guest would you speak to first? Who needs the most help in your opinion?

In my opinion, the first guest in this situation that will need help is Guest A. This person does not have a menu in front of them and they have not been talked to at all. A person is this situation will become frustrated if they are not spoken to quickly. Guest B and Guest C have both been helped to some degree so they are in less need of immediate attention than Guest A. They should be your first stop.

Guest B would be the next guest that needs help. They have not ordered and are looking at the menu. They will want to order soon. Guest C seems happy and is reading their paper.

To actually serve all of these guests, go to Guest A first and greet them. Offer them menus and take a drink order. Next help Guest B and take their order. Lastly, stop by Guest C and make sure that everything is perfect. If it is appropriate, offer them a refill on their beverage.

As a rule, each time you walk around your bar, take stock of each guest. Look at them and make sure that they seem OK. In many cases it will be obvious. If they are having a pleasant conversation or reading a newspaper, leave them alone. If you have not talked to a guest in a while, or they make eye contact with you, ask how they are doing and make sure things are going smoothly. Also, if you cannot get to someone right away, swing by and let them know you will be right with them as soon as possible. In general, if a guest knows they have been seen and you will be with them soon, they will patiently wait for a few minutes.

These rules and the idea of triage will help you very much with your guest service. I use them every time I am behind the bar and I suggest you do the same.

Walk-Up Service Program

Beyond the bartop, a bartender will often be responsible for the rest of the guests in the bar as well. However, you will often find guests in a bar do not sit and stay put like they would in a restaurant. People in a bar tend to move around. This is especially true of bars that have entertainment like video poker, video games,pinball, pool tables, shuffleboard or darts.

This makes keeping track of guests in this kind of environment very difficult. The simple way to deal with this problem is to not keep track of the guests. Instead, many bars choose to run tabs for people and let them come to the bar when they want more drinks or food. This type of service is often called a "walk-up" bar.

When a guest first comes to the bar and orders a drink, as them if they want to start a tab. If they do, start the tab using the policies of your bar. If they do not, simply take payment for each and every order that they make. Many people will not want to start a tab. They are often afraid that they will spend too much money or leave their collateral behind.

Walk-up bar service does not have the rigid steps that serving people who are sitting at the bar does. All you really need to do is keep their tabs up to date and make the drinks that they order. Usually the guest will wait while you are making the drinks and then take them back to where they are sitting or standing. Now that is not to say that you cannot take things to them. When I work in a situation like this, I will often run food out to them when it is ready. I will also make sure they have everything they need. However, as a rule, once they have everything, I will leave them alone until they come to the bar and ask for something else.

When the guest is done, they will need to come to the bar and settle their tab. Also as a rule, you should not go looking for people. This can leave your bar with liquor and your tip jar exposed to theft. This is not good for you or the bar.

Happy Hours

The hours between when lunch ends and dinner begins are the slowest hours in the bar and restaurant industry. To combat these slow hours, many bars offer a happy hour.

A happy hour (often several hours), is a period when a bar offers discounted drinks and inexpensive food items. A happy hour can be a wildly successful marketing technique that often draws in large crowds of people, depending on the specials that are offered. It is often the case that people in the surrounding neighborhood will take their lunch breaks to coincide with a bar's happy hour. This also can help foster regular guests and improve a bar's bottom line.

Tips

Tips are one of the main reasons that anyone ever wants to go into bartending. I know that's why I started. That being said, it may seem odd that tips are only going to be mentioned in this short section of the book. This section is not about how to earn tips. In point of fact, this entire book is about how to earn tips and every page it contains tells you how to maximize the tips you will receive from guests.

This section is primarily concerned with how to handle the tips you are given and what to do with them while you are working. We will also briefly discuss tipping those who help you do your job and reporting your tip income to the Internal Revenue Service.

Bartenders will work in one of two ways. They will either work alone or in a team. If a bartender works alone, all the tips that they earn will be theirs. If, on the other hand a bartender is working with others in a team, tips are generally pooled.

Pooling tips is what happens when all the bartenders place their tips in a central fund and split them at the end of the shift. This is a very common practice in the industry and is an idea that you should be both comfortable with and willing to accept. Everyone works together and gets an equal share of the money.

Tips are left for bartenders in two ways. They are either thrown into a tip jar as the product of a walkup service experience, or they are left on the bartop after a dining experience. If money is left on the bar, it should be added to a tip jar quickly.

How your bar handles credit card tips will vary. It may be the case that the money is taken out of the cash register and placed in a tip jar. It also may be the case that credit card tips are added to your paycheck and you will not get them at the end of the shift.

There can be more than one tip jar in a bar. In fact, it is a good idea to have as many tips jars as are needed. You don't want a guest having to look around to find a tip jar. They will quickly give up and keep the money for themselves. Often, I will have two tip jars that guests can see and one behind the bar. If the jars that the guests can see get too full, I will take money out of them and put it in the jar behind the bar. This makes it look like you are making less money than you are and also lowers the chance of someone stealing your tip jar. <u>This can and does happen so always keep your tip jar fairly empty and keep an eye on it.</u> I also like to add a few dollars to a tip jar at the start of the night. I call these "seed dollars". If people see an empty jar or bucket, all kinds of garbage can find its way in there. Seed dollars let people know that the jar is for tips and nothing else. I always count how many seed dollars I put in a jar and at the end of the night, I take these dollars back before I split the tips.

Tipping Out

Tipping out is the process of passing on a part of the tips you receive to people that help you do your job. People that fit this description include cooks, hosts, barbacks, bussers and sometimes mangers.

To many people that are new to the service industry, the idea of tipping out some of the money they worked hard for all night can be hard to swallow. This is another industry standard practice that you will need to accept right now. You would not have been able to make the tips that you did without these people and they deserve a "piece of the action".

The amount of money that you need to tip out will be determined by the customs of the bar or restaurant that you work in. Each place will have its own rules and you should always tip out at least the minimum amount set by those rules. However, I commonly exceed these guidelines. If you become a bartender, you will be working in a cash industry where friends are of enormous value when you are working. Friends can always be bought with tips. Happy hosts will always seat you right away. Happy bussers will always take your dishes back quickly and regularly and happy cooks will always make sure your food gets bumped to the front of the line if you need it. Little favors like these can make you much more efficient. This means you can help and be tipped by more guests and make even more tips. Think about that when you are tipping out.

You will be expected to tip people that help you to do your job. On the flip side of the coin, you will often also be tipped by your coworkers. You will receive these tips for making drinks that servers then take to guests sitting at their tables. This takes time and energy, as well as skill, and it is customary to reward this with money.

The amount of money that you will be tipped by any serving staff varies widely and there is not an industry accepted standard, in my opinion. I have been required tip outs as high as 7.5% of all alcohol sales in some cases. This means for every $100 of alcohol a server sells; they would be required to tip the bartender $7.50. This can add up quickly if your restaurant sells $5000 in alcohol each Friday night!

Tips & Uncle Sam

The Internal Revenue Service (IRS) considers tips that are earned by employees of bars and restaurants as regular income that is subject to normal taxation. You should claim all tips that you take home with you at the end of the night as income. The IRS wants to help you to claim the right amount of tips and makes several information resources available. An eight page question and answer brochure can be found at http://www.irs.gov/pub/irs-pdf/p1872.pdf . I strongly suggest reading through and complying with the rules in this useful document.

A tip log is a great means of keeping track of your tips. This can be something simple like a spiral notebook. In this notebook, you can keep information such as when you earned tips, how much you made, how much you tipped out and who you tipped. In the event that you are subjected to a tip audit (this is where the IRS examines your sales and the amount of tips you claimed as income), this document will be amazingly useful.

Cleanliness

A clean bar is the most basic service that you can offer to any of your guests. If your bar is not clean, guests will get a bad feeling and will not return, if they stay in the first place. As a bartender, it is your duty to make sure that your bar is as clean as possible at all times. A common phrase in the industry is "If you have time to lean, you have time to clean." This phrase should become second nature if you are to be successful in this trade. Whenever you are not helping a guest or stocking the bar, you should have a rag in your hand cleaning something. Trust me there will always be something that needs cleaning.

Your first duty should always be any areas that are visible to the customer. In most cases this will mean the bartop. Most of the drinks you will serve will be sticky and liquids will always wind up on the bar either as drink rings or dribbles. Always have many rags that are soaked in bleach water or another accepted sanitizer stashed around the bar ready for use at a moments notice. You should never be more than an arms reach away from a rag.

Sanitizers & Bleach Buckets

A wet rag is useless if it is only soaked in water. This does nothing more than spread stickiness around and leaves many germs unharmed. This is totally unacceptable. To be effective a rag needs to be soaked in a sanitizing solution. In most cases, a sanitizing solution is bleach mixed with cold water. Follow your local health department's regulation regarding the specific mixture. This is a perfectly effective and inexpensive sanitizing solution. Never mix bleach with hot water. This will cause the bleach to evaporate and the mix to become useless. Even mixing bleach with cold water, only slows this evaporation. To remain effective, the bleach solution should be changed regularly.

To combat the evaporation of bleach in water, many companies are switching over to more durable sanitizers. These chemicals are offered by many manufacturers and vary quite a bit. Their main attractions are the fact that these chemicals are often more gentle to human skin than bleach and the chemicals do not evaporate from water when they are in solution. If your bar uses chemicals of this type, always follow the manufacturer's directions for mixing and use.

Sanitizing solutions should be kept in "bleach buckets" stashed through out the bar. These are used to rewet rags that have dried out and are a very important part of the sanitizing system. Again, these should be very conveniently located and you should not be able to walk more than about ten feet without running across one.

Bussing

Cleaning up after your guests will be another very common task that you perform as a bartender. There are two forms of bussing that you should know. These are pre-bussing and post-bussing.

Pre-bussing is when you remove dishes that a guest has finished with. Ideally, this is done after each course that a guest has. For example, remove the empty soup bowl before the salad arrives and remove the empty salad plate before the entrée arrives. Also remove empty glasses each time you deliver a refill.

Post-bussing is when you remove everything that a guest used once they have finished and have left their seat at the bar. This should be done right after the guest has left. This is a good idea for two reasons. First, other guests sitting at your bar do not want to look at a mess while they are enjoying their cocktails or meals. Also, no new tipping guests will sit down at a dirty mess. To get more guests and make as much money as you can you always need to buss your tables in a hurry.

Neatness

Guests are not the only people in a bar that can make a mess. Many bartenders (I am in this category) can make quite a mess when they are mixing drinks. Fruit slices, juice dribbles, and beer slop can get everywhere when you are working. In reality, there is little that you can do to stop this from happening. What is more important is that you clean up after yourself as you go. Never leave everything messy and think that you can just clean it up at the end of the night. Never sacrifice customer service to clean, but clean as you go and do your best to keep your bar neat. Your guests and your coworkers will appreciate the effort.

Another area of neatness is garbage cans. A lot of trash is generated from mixing drinks. Always empty these cans whenever they get full. Only a poor bartender will let the garbage cans start overflowing.

Bathrooms

Bathroom cleaning will often be the responsibility of the bartender. If cleaning a urinal makes you squeamish, get over it or consider another career.

Whenever you clean the bathroom, scrub all the fixtures using an appropriate cleaning product and a good brush. A properly cleaned bathroom should have no hard water build up or stained toilets. Also make sure that you keep your bathrooms stocked with toilet paper, soap and paper towels.

Another instance when you will need to clean the bathrooms is when someone vomits in them. I hate cleaning vomit. In fact, everyone does. The fact that you will need to clean vomit is another fact that you need to come to grips with. I got used to it an you will too. One trick that helps you get over the smell, which is the worst part, is to rub a little Vick's™ VapoRub under your nose. This is a cold treatment that releases strong menthol vapors. These have a powerful smell that will overcome any other smell including vomit.

Once you are protected from the smell you can get down to cleaning. Before touching anything, protect yourself from any body fluids by making use of medical grade latex gloves. Any bar should have these. These will protect you from any blood or vomit born disease.

The easiest way to clean vomit is to use a vomit solidifier, which is a pink substance that absorbs liquids and turns into a paste. If your bar does not have this, cat litter works great too. Pour some on the vomit and wait a minute. Then carefully remove the solid mess form the floor. Then sanitize the area with a heavy duty sanitizer. Again, bleach works very well.

Personal Hygiene

Cleanliness and neatness do not stop with just your bar. Keeping yourself clean is also an important step for the professional bartender. Always shower before any shift that you work and always wear deodorant. Also, if you do not have a full beard, shave before you show up to work.

I also often will have an extra shirt with me when I work. Those spilled juices and sauces do not always wind up on the bar and you can easily wind up with a huge mess on you. If you do wind up dirty, get someone to cover your bar and change your shirt. One way to help solve this problem is to wear dark colors and bright patterned shirts if you can choose your own uniform. Shirts of these types do a very good job of hiding messes. Never wear white unless you have to.

Teamwork

Working as a bartender will often require you to work with other people. Actually, as a rule, a bartender is never alone in a bar. This would just be too much of a safety risk and there will almost always be a cook, a server or another bartender working with you. This means that you are going to have to know how to work with other people and get along to be a successful bartender.

Being polite to the people that you work with is the number one thing that you can do to help ensure that you are successful. Just like your mother used to say, always make sure to include your "please" and "thank you" when talking to other people. This little courtesy is always appreciated and will foster a friendly environment to work in.

This is especially true when the bar is busy. Busy times such as lunch and dinner can be very stressful and people are likely to snap at each other when they are under stress. Again, always keep your cool. Do not be polite to the guests when they can see you and rude to your co-workers when you are behind the scenes. This is just bad business. In reality, you are far more involved with your co-workers and their opinion of you matters just as much as the tipping guests.

If you happen to violate the principles laid out in the preceding paragraph, always apologize as soon as possible. When you are wrong, admit that you were out of line and ask for forgiveness. This again will go a great length in making sure that your bar remains harmonious and profitable for all. Hurt feelings and reluctance to apologize are just poison to this idea.

Behind the bar, space is often limited. This causes a number of problems that you should be aware of. Firstly, you are liable to run into your co-workers on more than one occasion. You are going to need to learn how to dance around each other and stay out of each others way in this type of a cramped environment.

To help your coworkers to move around you, try to let them know where you are. Never assume that you have been seen. If you are moving behind a coworker who is making a drink, say "Behind" good and loud. This will tell them not to back up suddenly and spill the drink they have worked hard to make. Hopefully, they will do the same to you. If they are taking an order and you do not want to interrupt, just put your hand on their back to let them know not to back up as well. Over time, if you work with the same people for a while, you will develop a rhythm that allows you to move around each other seamlessly. When this develops it makes working very easy and is often fun to watch.

There is no such thing as too much communication between team members. Make sure that you talk to each other all the time. Never be afraid to ask for help. Always make sure that everyone knows what their responsibility is. For example, often when two bartenders are working in a busy bar, one will make all of the server's drinks while the other tends to the bartop. In this case, both bartenders need to know that they are in charge of each operation. Never say something like "We can each just help each other." In past experiences this never works. Say something like "I will make the server drinks and you will take care of guests that sit at the bar." This is much more concrete and effective.

The last bit of advice that I want to pass on with regards to teamwork is to help your co-workers out as much as you can. This will often become a two way street and can be a real benefit to you as well. If you ever see a partner who looks rushed, or in a hurry or even panicking, ask them what you can do for them. If the other bartender is changing a keg and food comes up for one of their guests, do not hesitate to take it to the guest and treat them just as if they were yours. Make sure everything is perfect.

Closing Up

After working a long hard shift, you will be required to close up the bar and go home. Personally, I love a bar after hours. When you have worked in bars for a long time you will begin to associate them with a loud fast paced environment full of guest's that need things. At the end of the night when the doors are locked, the silence can be shocking and at the same time, relaxing. All of the guests are satisfied and it is time to count up the money. Trust me, when you experience it, you will know what I am talking about.

The first thing many bars do before closing is a last call. This is not mandatory and is often decided by the bartender. A last call is when you announce, either with a loud speech or to each guest individually that the bar will soon be closing and anyone who wishes to order one last drinks should do so now. If the crowd is lively and a little out of control, many bartender's will not do a last call but simply stop serving any more drinks. Last calls are usually done about ten minutes before the bar closes. This will give you enough time to prepare any drinks that are ordered.

Once you have done last call and before you close and lock the doors, you will need to get any guests that remain to leave. Never rush them out the door. Never put up chairs around them or turn of the music in the bar. This can hurt your tips and leave the guests feeling unwanted. Let them finish their drinks in a natural fashion. I am not telling you to let them sit their all night while you are just waiting but give them an appropriate amount of time.

Most people will leave in that reasonable amount of time. However, some guests will not. In this situation, you will need to politely ask them to leave. Do tell them to "Get Out." I generally prefer a speech like this:

"Sorry to say folks, but we are just about done here and I have to ask you guys to finish your drinks and move along."

This will get the job done in most cases. One special situation that you need to be aware of is guests who have had too much to drink. Always tell them that you would be happy to call them a cab and make every effort to prevent drunken customers from getting behind the wheel. If a drunken guest insists on driving, do not try to stop them physically. Instead follow the laws of your community. This often means calling the police and making a notation in the bar's log. We will talk more about intoxicated guests in the next chapter.

Once everyone is out, take care of the money and cleaning. How you deal with the money will be determined by the bar that you work in. You may simply turn your money into the manager and get to take your tips home. They will count the bank and the cash and do all the accounting. You may need to put the amount you were given as a bank back in a bag and turn that in with the money you received in another bag. You may not even need to talk to a manager, but instead, leave everything in a drop safe for the accounting department. A drop safe is a safe similar to a mailbox that has a slot for deposits. The contents of which can be accessed only with a combination. This type of setup is common in large businesses such as hotels and resorts.

As for cleaning, always do the best job that you can to leave the bar in good condition. Always make the bar look like you would like to see it first thing in the morning. Wipe away and drink circles and stickiness on the bar. Put away any items that need to be refrigerated, etc. If you do this, hopefully your coworkers will return the favor.

Always before you leave, if you are responsible for these items, make sure the safes are locked and all the money is put away, all cooking appliances are turned off and all doors are locked and any security system is armed. Most employers will forgive little things like a gallon of milk left out overnight. None will forgive you burning down their restaurant, money getting stolen or doors left open resulting in theft or vandalism.

Conclusion

The concepts outlined in this chapter will give you the basic working knowledge to be able to step behind a bar as a rookie bartender when combined with product knowledge and cocktail mixing skills.. Every bar that you work in will be different and do things in different ways. Be flexible and always approach any new situation with an open mind and a willingness to learn. Try not to get set in your ways and be willing to adapt. This will be a very helpful ability. Remember that the strongest plant in nature is the reed because, although it will always bend because of its flexibility, it will never break.

Homework Assignment # 2 – Visit A Bar Again

Instead of review questions, this chapter ends with another homework assignment. Again, I am going to ask you to visit a bar and do some observation. Unlike the last time you were asked to visit a bar, I am going to set some guidelines this time. The bar that you sit at should have seating along the bartop. This will allow a very good vantage point to watch the bartenders while they are working. Also the bar should have a happy hour that is popular and serves food.

You will need to visit the bar between 4:00 and 6:00 PM. This time period will include the end of a happy hour in most cases, shift change, the beginning of the busy dinner period.

I want you to observe the bartenders again. As before, if you are not discreet, you will be asked to leave. Take a friend or a newspaper. This will make it less obvious that you are observing. Watch and see how the bartender's interact with each other and what they do. Remember what you have read in this chapter and look for the habits and procedures I have described.

Homework Questions

1. What kind of service did this bar offer? Walk-up? Bartop service?

2. Did they require tabs or did the bartenders need to keep track of everyone?

3. Did you see any stocking going on? What did you see?

4. How many bartenders were working? Were they sharing responsibilities? How were these divided?

5. Were the bartenders helping each other? How were they doing this?

6. What kind of communication was going on? Describe what you saw and heard.

Chapter 8
Responsible Bartending

Bartending can be a lot of fun, however, a bartender has lots of responsibilities to their guests, the bar itself, the community as a whole and to themselves. In this chapter we are going to discuss steps that you need to take in order to protect yourself and everyone else around you. Take these matters very seriously when you are working. Failure to do so can result in serious injury, life altering problems, and lawsuits.

Alcohol Education

Many of the states in America require people who serve alcohol in a public venue to undergo some kind of alcohol education. This is one of the first things you will need to do before you can seek employment as a bartender.

To find and comply with your state's regulations regarding alcohol serving, you will need to contact your state agency that regulates alcohol. Most often, you will need to take a class that lasts several hours, as well as pass a test and pay a fee. These requirements are not terribly difficult and all you need to do is pay attention to the instruction and to take the matter seriously and you should be fine.

In the next few pages, this book is going to discuss alcohol the drug, alcohol and the body and intoxication. These discussions are not intended to replace formal alcohol education but only to explain basic concepts. When working as a bartender always comply with the laws of your community and follow all of your employer's procedures. These have been set forth to protect society, the bar, the guest and you; the bartender.

Alcohol The Drug

Alcohol is actually a class of chemicals. Referring to the active ingredient of vodka as alcohol is not technically correct. The specific type of alcohol that is intended for human consumption is known as "ethanol". Other types of alcohol include methanol, a solvent, and propanol or rubbing alcohol that is used as an antiseptic. Only ethanol is consumed by humans as the others can lead to serious ailments if not death when consumed. Ethanol is made up of two atoms of Carbon, six atoms of Hydrogen and a single atom of Oxygen.

Ethanol acts on the body as a depressant on the central nervous system (i.e. the brain) and slows down the brain's ability to carry on certain functions. This and other chemical reactions are what lead to the state of intoxication associated with alcohol. Alcohol is actually a mildly toxic chemical whose effects are often pleasing to the drinker. Compared to other members of the alcohol chemical family, the toxicity of ethanol is actually pretty low.

Alcohol can also be metabolized by the body as a food source. This means that alcohol is actually treated as a food by the body.

In the body, ethanol is processed by the liver which acts as the bodies filter and removes toxins from the blood stream. The amount of alcohol that the liver can remove from the blood per hour is fairly low and if a person is drinking heavily, a build up of alcohol occurs in the body and causes intoxication. A normal human liver can remove the amount of alcohol contained in a 12 ounce beer, a 5 ounce glass of wine or 1.25 ounces of hard alcohol per hour.

The liver can be damaged by excessive drinking of alcohol over long periods resulting in large fatty deposits on the liver. This is known as "fatty liver". Over time, scarring, known as cirrhosis, can also occur resulting in reduced liver function and even liver failure.

Intoxication

People will often consume more alcohol than their body can remove per hour. This creates a state known as intoxication. For the purposes of this book, intoxication will be described as the state when body functions are impaired from the consumption of alcoholic beverages. This includes a loss of judgement as well as the loss of balance.

This presents many challenges for a bartender. People who are intoxicated can have accidents and hurt themselves, become combative and start fights, and become ill as well. All of these consequences of alcohol consumption are negative. Detecting and managing intoxicated gusts is a huge part of being a responsible bartender.

There are many signs when a person has become intoxicated. Some of these signs are:

- Slurred Speech
- Red In The Face
- Poor Balance or Trouble Standing
- Aggressive Behavior

- Improper Sexual Advances
- Spilling Things
- Trouble Sitting Still
- Drowsiness
- Loud or Crude Language
- Trouble Communicating Ideas
- Arguing With The Bartender
- Falling Asleep

Someone who has reached a state of intoxication will often display one if not several of these behaviors. In most states, you are required by law to stop serving an individual who has reached a state of intoxication.

Intoxication is legally determined by measuring the amount of alcohol that is present in a person's blood. This is called the Blood Alcohol Level or BAL. It used to be required that a person submit blood to determine their BAL. However, with the advent of new technologies, BAL can be measured using a unit known as a breathalyzer. This unit simply requires a person to breathe into it to determine an accurate BAL. In most areas, a BAL of .08% or above is considered legally intoxicated. However, it is completely possible for a person to be showing all the signs of intoxication at a lower BAL. Since you will not be able to measure BAL in the bar, again rely on watching for visible signs of intoxication.

Spotting someone who is intoxicated can be difficult at times. Many times a person who is intoxicated will be able to pull themselves together and hide the symptoms of their intoxication long enough to order another drink. The best way to spot someone who is intoxicated is to engage them in conversation. You don't need to interrogate them. Simply talk to them about something simple for a minute or two and watch them while you do it. If they are intoxicated, a few minutes of talking will be enough to reveal the signs.

It is very important to note that there is no way to sober up a person who is intoxicated. Coffee, water and hot sauces do not work. The only way to sober a person up is to allow the liver enough time to process all of the alcohol out of their blood. While it will not sober a person up, offering them water is a great thing to do for an intoxicated guest. Alcohol causes dehydration in the body and adding water to their system will help lessen any hangover they have in the morning.

It is also very important to note that intoxication may not result only form the alcoholic drinks that you serve a guest. Many medications interact poorly with alcohol and can cause unexpected results. You have no idea what kind of medications a guest may have taken before they walked into your bar. Additionally, this person may have been drinking at home before they came to your bar or may have just come from another bar up the street. This means that they only way you can determine the person's current state of intoxication is to, again, engage them in conversation and to look for signs of intoxication.

Alcohol Tolerance

People who engage in heavy drinking on a frequent basis will develop a tolerance to the effects of alcohol. This tolerance can allow them to consume alcohol without showing the signs of intoxication that would otherwise become obvious. However, as the person continues to drink, their BAL continues to rise. Even if a person is not showing the signs of intoxication, but their BAL is above the legal limit, they are considered intoxicated.

In this kind of a situation, all you can do is rely on your best judgment and observe the amount of alcohol your guests are consuming. If a person consumes six shots in the span of 5 minutes, for example, you know that their liver can only process out one of those shots in the next hour. In this situation, it is entirely possible that the guest's BAL is above the legal limit. In this situation, it would be irresponsible to continue serving the guest. When you believe a guest is intoxicated regardless of whether or not they are showing signs of intoxication, they are. In a situation like this it is much better to error on the side of caution and stop service than to operate in a reckless manner.

To combat this problem, many bars will have house maximums that detail how many drinks a person may have. This helps to limit the amount of alcohol that can be served to a guest on the premises.

Keeping A Liquor Log

Every bar in the country maintains a liquor incident log. This log is simply the official record of all events of note that involved liquor. Examples of events that should be noted in the log include:

- Cut Offs

- When You Pull A Drink

- People Without Proper ID

- When You Call A Cab For An Intoxicated Guest

- Intoxicated Guests Who Refused A Cab

- Anytime The Police Are Called

You should write in this log each and every time you work. Even if nothing noteworthy happens write something like "No Liquor Incidents". If something does happen, make sure you are specific and include as many details as possible. Sadly, you have no idea when this book will be requested by the police, an attorney or liquor control agents. Your documentation is your official record and offers you a degree of legal protection. Being specific and factual is essential.

I also strongly recommend that you keep a personal liquor incident log as well, in addition to the bar's. This will serve as a backup record in the event that you no longer work at the bar in question when the log is requested or in the event that the primary log is lost. Where legal documentation and protections are concerned, you can never have too much.

Cutting Off A Guest

There are many ways to deal with an intoxicated guest to ensure that they, the bar and you all remain safe. The very first thing that you should do when you discover one of your guests is intoxicated is to stop serving them. This will also show that you were not recklessly serving people. This seems basic but may people that work in bars are reluctant to stop serving, or "cut off" a guest. They will often be afraid of how the guest will react. This is a fear that you will need to overcome.

Many people prefer to ignore a guest's request and keep them from getting a drink. I am not a fan of this technique. It leaves the guest in doubt of what is happening. In my experience, the best way to cut someone off it to simply say, **"I am not going to be able to serve you any more alcohol. Can I grab you a non-alcoholic beverage?"** This tells the guest what is going on. You can take this a step further and tell them this while you hand them a cup of coffee. In many case, this will be taken as a signal to the guest that you have decided they are intoxicated.

Never tell a guest that you think they are "drunk". This can be embarrassing to a guest and will often make them argumentative. Also, never argue with a guest. You are in charge. If you have decided that they are intoxicated and you will not serve them anymore, stick to your guns.

Another good technique that will help you in a cut off situation is to find someone sober in the intoxicated person's party to help you. They often have more influence and will be respected by the intoxicated person more than you. For example one brother talking to another who is intoxicated can often have a calming effect on a situation. In the event you choose to make use of this technique, pull the sober person aside and explain the situation to them. Ask for their help. They will often help you and make the process of cutting someone off much smoother.

Guest's will often supply you with excuses that explain that they are not drunk. My personal favorite is when someone tells me that they are not drunk, instead they had just smoked marijuana. Well that is still intoxicated and they are not getting another drink. Don't let someone tell you that they have a speech impediment, are a diabetic, or have an accent from New York. If you carefully looked for the signs and you believe they are intoxicated do not serve them any more.

Any time that you cut a person off, make sure you include documentation of the incident in the official log. Also make sure you communicate and let any other employees who can serve alcohol know that the person is cut off. Your efforts are wasted if the intoxicated person can simply go to another bartender and get another drink.

Pulling A Drink

Many states have laws that say once a guest begins to show signs of intoxication, you as the bartender are required to make a "good faith" effort to take the drink away from the guest. In the industry this is known as "pulling a drink".

Let's first define a "good faith effort". This means that you make every attempt to take the drink away from the guest, **short of physically taking it.** Never try to take a glass by physical force from a guest. This will often create an aggressive environment that can lead to a fight and injury. This is something that should always be avoided. If the guest resists your effort to take the drink let them finish it and do not serve them anymore. If the guest stops you from taking their drink, make sure that you document this point in your liquor log as well.

The best way to pull a drink is to walk up when the drink is not in the guest's hand and simply take it. Explain what you are doing when the drink has been moved out of the guest's reach. Again, try to be discrete. Embarrassing a guest in front of their friends is a sure fire way to cause a bigger problem. I will, again, always offer to provide a nonalcoholic drink. If your bar's rules allow it, provide it free of charge. Also, if your bar's rules allow it, provide a refund for the pulled drink when appropriate.

Pulling a drink from a guest and properly documenting it, will again show that you are serving alcohol in a responsible manner and are making every effort to ensure everyone's safety.

Sober Drivers

With an intoxicated guest, the last thing you want to do is let them get behind the wheel of their car and go hurt someone. To prevent this from happening, you need to be prepared to make sure that a sober driver drives the intoxicated person somewhere safe.

If there is a designated driver in the group to which the guest belongs, speak to them and make sure that the intoxicated person is in their charge.

If there is not a designated or sober driver in the group, declare that you are going to call them a cab. Don't ask, just make the statement. If the guest does not have enough money to pay for the cab, it is better that your bar pay for it than let the person get behind the wheel of a car. Most of the time the guest will agree with you and they appreciate your concern. You should have the telephone number of several cab companies in your area memorized and ready to use when you need them. On weekend nights one company may have a busy signal, if that is the case call another. When you speak to the operator, inform them that you are the bartender and you need a cab for a guest. Give them your name so the cabbie can find you when they arrive.

It can also take a while for a cab to actually arrive. Be prepared to keep the guest busy while they wait. The last thing that you want to happen is for them to grow tired of waiting for their cab and decide to sneak out and drive. Keep an eye on them and offer them complimentary nonalcoholic beverages. Don't let them pass out. This can be dangerous and looks bad for the bar. When the cab arrives, help them in and make sure they are able to provide the cab driver with directions.

If you believe an intoxicated person is going to drive, call the police. It is better that a person be taken to detox rather than allowing them to injure themselves or others by driving. It is your job as the bartender to prevent an intoxicated guest from getting behind the wheel of a car. An intoxicated guest should only leave your bar with a designated driver, a cab driver, or the police. Again, where safety is concerned it is better to error on the side of caution.

Alcohol & Pregnancy

Expectant mothers who consume alcohol during pregnancy run the risk of giving birth to babies that suffer from Fetal Alcohol Syndrome or FAS.

FAS is a condition where a baby is born with a damaged nervous system, especially the brain. In milder forms, FAS results in children with poor mental faculties and attention deficit problems.

Many new bartenders are concerned with having to serve a pregnant woman alcohol. This can be a sensitive subject. As a rule, you should not ever refuse service to a woman that you think is pregnant. Firstly, you could be wrong about her being pregnant. This will often present a very bad situation. Additionally, you can be sued on the basis of discrimination for having refused service to a pregnant woman as well.

Any way that you slice this situation, it is best to do nothing and provide the drink as requested. One fact that might add comfort to your conscience is that it is not known how much alcohol or when the baby is exposed to it will cause FAS.

Carding

Along with managing intoxicated guests, one of the most important responsibilities of a bartender is to prevent minors from receiving and consuming alcohol. In the United States, it is a national standard that persons under 21 years of age may not legally consume alcohol.

In many communities, serving a minor is considered a misdemeanor and will result in fines as high as $10,000 and possible jail time. Almost every employer will immediately fire you. Additionally, you may be blocked from working as a bartender in the future. That is right, along with an enormous fine, you are out of work and have no income to pay the fine as well as possibly having to do time in jail. It is that serious. Please never take a chance with this situation it is just not worth the risk!

Acceptable Identification

Many times when a guest orders a drink, you will need to ask for identification that verifies that they are old enough to legally consume it. However, you are going to need to know what forms of identification you can accept.

The forms of ID that you can accept will be determined by your place of employment. However, as a general rule you will be able to accept only the following IDs:

- National or State Issued Identification Card

- State Issued Driver's License

- Passport

- Military Identification Card

Every bar in business should have a comprehensive identification guide. This guide should show, in color, each and every form of ID that is common in the United States and Canada. Additionally, each ID's features are discussed in detail. These guides may be purchased at www.driverslicenseguide.com. This is a good resource to have.

A state issued identification card is simply a card that bears information and a photograph of the bearer. The card should have a unique identifying number along with birth date, address, height, weight, and eye color. Along with this information, the identification card will also have an expiration date. Beyond this date, the ID is not valid and should not be accepted. Some states, such as Arizona, have identification cards that only expire the person's 65th birthday. Examples of this type of ID include a Wyoming driver's license or a Permanent Resident card issued by the federal government.

Additionally, in response to the Patriot Act and the requirement of passports or birth certificates to cross back from Canada and Mexico into the United States, many states are beginning to offer "Enhanced Identification Cards". These cards look similar to existing identification cards but have additional information and security features that make them acceptable for crossing international borders.

Wyoming and Rhode Islands are states. However, "state" can also mean Great Britain and Korea as well. These are also acceptable forms of identification. However, with foreign issued ID cards you need to be a little more careful. First, you should only accept the ID if you can read the language in which the card is printed. If you are presented with a Korean ID card and you do not read Korean, do not accept the ID. Secondly, you should be comfortable with the authenticity of the ID. You can also buy international ID guides from www.driverslicenseguide.com. If you are at all suspicious or uncomfortable with an ID, simply refuse service.

Another common form of ID card in the United States is the "Matricula Consular". This form of ID card is issued by the Mexican Government through its consulates and embassies outside of Mexico. The purpose of this ID card is to offer a means of Mexican Government identification to Mexican citizens who are living outside the territorial boundaries of Mexico. This ID is printed in both Spanish and English to make it useful in the United States. Many bars will not accept these cards. If you have questions, ask your manager before accepting a Metricula Consular.

A driver's license is a state issued ID card that allows a person the privilege of driving a car within the United States. This is the most common form of identification that you will see while working as a bartender. This identification has all of the characteristics that are found on a state issued ID card including birth date, expiration date, weight, gender, hair and eye color and address. Included on a deriver's license is also a photograph of the person to whom the license belongs.

After state issued ID cards and driver's licenses, the next most common form of ID you will see in the bar is a passport. A passport is a piece of identification that is issued by the national government of the bearer's country. This form of identification is intended to be used in the owner's country as well as when traveling abroad and crossing international boundaries.

A passport is not a single card like state issued ID cards. Instead a passport is a booklet that contains many pages. When opened, the front cover of a passport will contain a photograph of the bearer as well as their birth date. Personal information such as address, weight, eye and hair color, are not included in a passport. Gender information is also included.

A person presenting you with a passport as their form of identification will often not be a citizen of the United States. It is also likely that you will not be able to read the language of the person's native country. Fortunately, most passports are printed in the native language of the issuing country, French and, most importantly, English. This will allow you to read the ID most of the time. If for some reason the passport is not printed in English (very unlikely) and you cannot read it, do not accept it.

One thing to consider when accepting a passport as ID is that passports are often issued for periods as long as ten years. This means that someone presenting a passport to you when they are 21 may have been issued the passport with a current photo when they were 11. I know that my picture when I was 21 and when I was 11 were very different. In this sort of a situation, backup ID (to be discussed shortly) is highly recommended.

The last piece of commonly accepted ID in the United States is a U.S. Military ID. This piece of ID is issued to all members of the United States armed service and Defense Department civilian contractors and is considered their official identification.

This form of ID contains a picture, rank information, pay grade, which service the bearer belongs to, along with several barcodes and a gold integrated circuit chip. The expiration date of the ID is listed on the front of the ID.

The birth date on current military IDs is located on the back of the card on a second black and white photo of the bearer. Flip it over and check it before you do anything else when you are presented with a military ID.

Backup ID

The forms of ID that were described in the preceding section are the only forms of ID that you should ever accept. However, in some cases, a secondary form of ID is needed *in addition* to these forms.

Many times ID will be cracked or broken. In the cases that I have mentioned of people using passports from when they were 11 or in the case of the Arizona ID, people may have changed from the picture shown. This can create a risk that the person presenting the ID is not the owner of the ID. Asking for a second piece of ID can help assure you that this person is the one on the ID. A person using their older brother's ID will not have a bank card with their brother's name. Asking for backup ID is a great way to eliminate this risk.

Secondary ID does not need to be as exclusive as the primary ID. It does not have to be issued by a government organization. Some great examples of backup ID include:

- Bank cards including ATM, debit and credit cards
- Insurance cards
- Student ID
- Work identification cards
- Birth certificate
- Social security card

It is very rare to find a person out on the town without one of these forms of identification on them. In the event you are unsure of the primary ID and the person cannot produce a second form of ID, error on the side of caution and refuse service. It is not worth the risk.

When To Ask For ID

As I have said, in the United States, the legal drinking age in all fifty states is 21. First and foremost, anyone who looks under the age of 21 should immediately prompt an ID request.

However, in my experience as a bartender I have often been surprised at how poorly a judge of age I am. People who look 16 to me are really 25 and women who look 30 are often 40. This can create a real problem and can lead to not carding when you need to.

To protect you and to protect the bar or restaurant, many companies require their employees to request ID of any patron who looks under the age of 40. Some companies require that anyone who orders an alcoholic drink be carded, no matter what their apparent age, even if the are celebrating their 100th birthday. Always follow the policies as set by the company that you work for. These are often more strict than state laws and exist to protect you as well as the company.

Anytime someone orders a very fruity drink that hides the flavor of alcohol, stop and give them a good look and ask yourself if they look over 40. Young people are unaccustomed to the flavor of alcohol and will try and cover it up with sweet fruit juices. Another red flag is when someone wastes premium liquor that is more appropriate for sipping, with a mixer or in an odd combination. An example of this would be premium tequila mixed with cola. A person with a lot of experience drinking will not order this drink. Anyone who does should make you stop and evaluate their age and consider carding.

You should also take the guests into consideration when thinking about carding someone. Who is at the bar? If three of your four guests look under 21 and the fourth does not, card them all. It is possible the fourth person is the same age but has developed faster. Also, if you have four women guests and you **need** to card three of them, just card everyone. The woman you leave out will never forgive you for making her feel like the one old woman at the table.

In reality, anytime you have even the slightest doubt that someone is under the age of 21 do not hesitate for one second to request their ID.

How To Card Someone

Carding someone for the first time can be an intimidating experience. There is a set procedure that you need to follow. However, once you have memorized this process you simply need to follow it every time and use your best judgment to be successful.

First and foremost, always make sure the person you will be serving is standing or sitting in front of you when you look over their ID. Never look over someone's ID if the are parking the car, in the bathroom, or finishing their cigarette. If they are not there and their friend is trying to present their ID, politely tell them you will wait until they have returned.

Once the person is in front of you, politely ask to see their ID. **Some nice ways to ask for your ID are**:

- I have not had the privilege of your ID. Do you mind?
- Can I please take a quick look at your ID?
- You mind if I see your ID?

Bad ways to request ID would be:

- Give me your ID.
- I am not serving you until I see your ID.

The guest will then present you with their ID. Many times they will try to show you their ID still in their wallet. Politely ask them to take the ID out of the wallet so you can hold it.

This is done for several reasons. First, many wallets will cover up essential information such as the expiration date. If you cannot see this information, you cannot verify that the ID is legitimate. Also, you need to be able to touch the ID to feel for laminate that may indicate an altered ID, or a thinness that may indicate a counterfeit ID. Many guests will complain that it is difficult to remove and ID from their wallet. Apologize but politely insist that they do it. If they refuse, you will have to refuse service.

Additionally, if your bar employs a barcode/magnetic scanner you will need to have the ID out of the wallet to run it through this device. These devices present the information encoded on U.S. IDs to the bartender for comparison to the information printed on the front of the ID. This is a great check against altered IDs, but they are expensive and not terribly common in bars yet.

Once the ID is in your hands, carefully study it. If it is dark and you cannot see well, use a flashlight There are three main points that you must look at and verify each time. These are:

- **Birth Date** – This is used to verify that the person is over the legal age of 21 and can legally consume alcohol. Carefully examine this and make sure that you know the current date each and every time you go to work.

- **Expiration Date** – Any ID used to prove someone's identification must not have expired to be considered valid. If an ID has expired it cannot be accepted as ID to drink no matter how old the person looks.

- **Photo** – Of course you need to make sure that the person presenting the ID looks like the person pictured on the ID itself. If an African American woman presents the ID of a Hispanic man, it would be best to refuse service.

Once you have examined the ID and compared it to the person who presented it, and are satisfied that the person is old enough to drink and is the owner of the ID, you can proceed with service. If you are still not comfortable request backup ID. If this is not forthcoming, refuse service.

Fake IDs

People who are under the legal age to drink will sometimes try to do so with ID that is not genuine. These forms of IDs are commonly called "fake IDs". While the movies and memories from high school may romanticize this practice, it is a serious matter. Bartenders who are fooled by these IDs can easily be fined and lose their jobs. To protect yourself against IDs of this kind, always be on your guard. Again, if you ever feel uncomfortable with an ID for any reason whatsoever, simply refuse service. Better to be safe than sorry.

Borrowed ID

The most common fake ID that you will encounter in a bar is borrowed ID. This is simply someone borrowing a friend or family members ID and pretending to be them to purchase alcohol. The person in the picture will generally resemble the person that is presenting it but careful inspection will reveal differences. Always study the IDs picture carefully and compare it to the person while they are in front of you.

This method of hiding one's identity requires the least amount of effort and no technological sophistication.

Altered ID

After borrowed IDs the next most likely form of fake ID will be an altered ID. This type of ID was a genuine state issued ID but has been altered in some way. The most commonly altered items are the birth date and the expiration date. Always study the type on the ID carefully. Does everything look the same? Run your finger over the ID and try to feel for any added laminates that may conceal the real information.

In the event that the birth date is changed, the person is under the legal age to drink and is trying to change their ID to make it appear that they are in fact old enough.

In the event that the expiration date has been changed, the ID is most likely a discarded ID from an older family member who has gotten a new ID. The younger family member who resembles their older brother or sister has changed the expiation date to make the ID look valid.

This method of faking an ID requires more sophistication and precision, this makes altered IDs less common than borrowed ID but a still frequent occurrence.

Counterfeit ID

Counterfeit IDs are the least common form of fake IDs that you will come across. These IDs require a great deal of sophistication and money to produce. The best way to catch these IDs is to examine the ID very carefully and compare it to an ID checking guide. Check and feel the weight of the plastic that the ID is printed on by bending it slightly. Does it feel normal? Also, is the ID the right size? Is this a current ID or is it the old fashioned, laminated kind?

Talking While You Are Carding

Your knowledge of IDs is very important. You should be familiar with many of the IDs in the United States and you should know what a legal, genuine ID feels like.

However, the best way to catch someone trying to pass off a fake ID is the exact same technique that you should use to discover when people are intoxicated. All you need to do is to talk to them and ask them questions.

The way to challenge someone when you are carding them is to ask questions to which they should know the answer. However, the answers to these questions should not be printed on the ID. The reason for this is, most likely, someone trying to pass off a fake ID will have memorized all of the information on the ID.

For example, do not ask their birth date. Instead, ask them how old they are. Someone's age is always changing and requires them to be constantly aware of how old they are. Someone who is presenting their real ID will have little trouble answering this question, but someone passing a fake ID may volunteer their real age, or make a blatant and obvious mistake. Better yet, they may try to calculate the answer in their head on the fly. All of these responses should be a dead give away and should result in you denying service.

Another very good question to challenge someone is to ask what their someone's astrological sign is. This, again, is something everyone knows. Someone passing a fake ID will most likely not know the proper answer to this question and again it will offer a quick check as to whether or not the ID is valid.

The astrological signs and their corresponding birth dates are as follows:

Aquarius January 20th – February 19th	**Leo** July 24th – August 23rd
Pisces February 20th – March 20th	**Virgo** August 24th – September 23rd
Aries March 21st – April 20th	**Libra** September 24th – October 23rd
Taurus April 21st – May 21st	**Scorpio** October 24th – November 22nd
Gemini May 22nd – June 22nd	**Sagittarius** December 23rd – Jan 19th
Cancer June 23rd – July 23rd	**Capricorn** December 23rd – January 19th

It would not be a bad idea to memorize these dates. If you have a bad memory, photocopy this page and keep it with you so you are ready to challenge an ID if necessary.

Confiscating Fake ID

Some bars make it a policy to confiscate fake IDs. The IDs are then turned into the local police department for pickup. The idea behind this is that no one who is passing off a fake ID would be dumb enough to try and go retrieve it form the police. By extension, less fake IDs will be on the street because of this policy.

I do not and never have agreed with policy. Yes, I do believe that it is a good idea to try and keep the number of fake IDs floating around to a minimum. However, I do not think taking them directly from the hands of a bar's guest is the best way to do it.

In the first place, taking an ID from someone raises the tension of the situation and makes it much more likely that a fight or some other violence will result. This is bad for business, the bar's image and possibly the bartender.

Additionally, what if you are wrong? Can you imagine how angry a person would be if their legitimate ID was confiscated from a bar and they were told they would need to pick it up from the police? This person will **NEVER** return to your bar and will tell everyone they know about the nightmare situation that you created for them

The best way to handle fake IDs is to simply refuse service. This does not create the risk of violence and if you are wrong about the ID, you only inconvenience the guest in a minor way. This should be your policy.

Minor Stings

To prevent the sale of alcohol to minors in bars, law enforcement agencies will run "minor stings". Minor stings are when an underage person, in partnership with a local law enforcement agency, tries to purchase alcohol from a vendor. This can occur in retail liquor outlets like grocery and liquor stores and in service environments like bars and restaurants.

The minor will always be accompanied by a law enforcement agent. This agent will witness the attempted purchase, incognito, and be able to verify all events in court. If you pass the sting attempt and refuse service, the law enforcement agent may congratulate you and inform you that you have passed. In the unfortunate event that you fail the sting, the law enforcement agent will issue fines and or arrest you! No matter what happens, either way, you should always follow all instructions from the law enforcement agent.

In any case, failing a sting will result in a fine and possible jail time for you as well as a possible fine for your employer. In most cases you will be fired and may lose the privilege of serving alcohol in the future.

The purpose of minor stings is to ensure compliance with state laws governing liquor sales. If you always follow the law and properly request ID and check ages, you have nothing to fear from a sting.

Calling Emergency Services

The best preparation that you can take for an emergency is know how to get help when you need it whether it be police, fire or medical services. In most areas of the United States, your local emergency dispatch can be reached at 911. This number should be right next to the house phone, as sometimes in an emergency people panic and forget the number.

Do not be afraid to call emergency services if you feel that they are needed. In a situation like that, it is always best to error on the side of caution and have too much help rather than too little. It is their job and they are glad to help you.

First Aid & CPR Training

Anyone walking into your bar can have a sudden and life threatening emergency. It could be a person drops down with a heart attack, someone has an allergic reaction to a food item and goes into shock and cannot breathe, or someone has been drinking and stumbles and breaks a leg. These are all entirely possible and you as the bartender should take steps to make sure that you are prepared to address these and any other situations that may arise.

To help in your preparation, your bar should be supplied with a well stocked industrial grade first aid kit. These kits offer more than just antiseptic, aspirin and bandages. Instead these kits offer cold compresses, industrial grade burn treatments and trauma bandages, as well as body fluid controls and CPR equipment. If you bar does not have this equipment, speak to the manager about making sure that you get one. If someone on the premises has an emergency you and the owner will be glad a kit of this type was present.

In addition to having the equipment that you will need, it is essential that you know how to use it. To acquire the training that you will need, find and take a first aid and CPR class. The best place to look for a class of this type is with your local chapter of the American Red Cross. This organization's website at http://www.redcross.org is a great resource and can direct you to programs in your area. Additionally, many community colleges offer a comprehensive industrial first aid class. This too will provide you with all the skills you need to help save a life during an emergency.

Safety Awareness

Other than knowing about 911, taking a first aid class, and knowing how to handle a fire your best line of defense is simply "safety awareness". This is where you are conscious of safety hazards and take the necessary steps to correct them.

For example, if a glass gets broken over the well, melt all the ice and clean out any and all broken glass. Glass can easily hide in ice and only properly melting, cleaning and inspecting the ice well can properly protect your guests. Do not just assume nothing fell in there.

Additionally, spills are a big problem in a bar. Always put down a "Wet Floor" sign right away and clean up the spill as quickly as possible to prevent injury.

If you can not get to these problems right away, ask someone to help you. Teamwork is especially important when we are talking about protecting employees and guests from serious injury.

Security

It is a sad fact that people go out, consume alcohol and start trouble. This might mean that they start fights or sexually harass bar staff. Due to this situation, you will need to maintain constant control of your bar environment. In this section we are going to discuss several security issues that relate specifically to bartenders.

Safety In Numbers

This is a fairly simple idea. Never be alone in the bar if you can avoid it. The buddy system worked when you went on field trips to the zoo and it is still valid when you are slinging drinks. Anyone who is in the mood to start trouble will often give it a second thought when they realize that there is more than one person with whom they will have to deal.

Your partner does not necessarily have to be another bartender. A cook, busboy, dishwasher, or host will all do. Do whatever is necessary to make sure someone else is around. If your manager or owner insists on your working alone, you may want to reconsider where you are working.

Controlling Guest Behaviors

The easiest way to prevent any trouble in your bar is to control the environment while you are working. Always observe and monitor all of your guests. Listen to what is being said. Put a stop to any and all offensive, racist or profane language before it becomes a problem.

Another common problem is unwanted attention form the opposite gender. In many cases, wine will go to a persons head and they miss obvious signals saying their advances are not welcome. If this is the case and your help is requested, offer whatever assistance you think is appropriate and make sure the guest remains comfortable and safe.

If a person does not listen to and adhere to your request to change their behavior, it is best if they leave the bar. Kicking someone out of your bar for the first time is even more intimidating than cutting someone off. My only advice is to politely ask them to leave in a firm tone. Always remain calm and keep your cool. They may try to make a scene or provoke you into a fight, but do not rise to the challenge. If they refuse to leave, call whatever security your bar may have or the police. They will handle the matter from there in accordance with local laws.

Fights

Fights happen in bars. This is a fact of life. Often, when people go out and drink, their inhibitions and judgment are diminished. This leads to cockiness and fights result. Be prepared to deal with these.

The best way to deal with a fight is with a booming voice. This will often be enough to startle the fighters into stopping. Try shouting something to the effect of:

"STOP NOW OR I AM CALLING THE COPS!"

Really shout this in a commanding voice. People take the police seriously and will generally stop for a minute. If any friends are around, they have a chance to step in and calmly break up the fight.

If this does not work, carry out your threat and call the police. While you are waiting for the police to arrive, you can try and break up the fight. This can be a dangerous proposal and can lead to your injury. Use a great deal of caution if you choose to break up a fight physically. I do not recommend it.

As a rule, everyone involved in a fight should be asked to leave the bar, if not arrested. If they stay, another fight may break out. Someone might go home and come back with a shotgun. You do not know. It is best if all those elements just leave the bar and do not return.

Doormen & Security Guards

Doormen are employees who watch the door of the bar and check IDs. The fact that doormen check IDs should never stop you from checking a guest's ID. It will not stop you from all the negative consequences of serving a minor.

Doormen also act as a security force for many bars. These men are generally large intimidating people who are used to convince would be trouble makers that they are better off leaving.

Whenever you are faced with people who are unruly or troublesome, a threat to call security is often more than enough to calm them down quickly.

I have never hesitated to make use of security guards when I am working. If there is a 300 pound man who is drunk and threatening, there is no reason to not have backup. Again, the presence of security guards will often calm down a situation very quickly. In the event that things get out of control and a fight develops, you will be glad that you called security and that they are there to help you.

Police

Police are great people. They go out everyday and put their lives on the line to protect average citizens. You will also greatly appreciate police when a situation gets out of control in your bar.

Never hesitate to call police if you think that they are needed. It is what they get paid to do and usually your instinct will prove right. Additionally, security guards are great, but police have the ability to use deadly force if needed. As such they have a chilling effect on many people and will restore order one way or the other.

Once the police arrive, offer them any assistance they require. Answer any question honestly, calmly and quickly and provide them with any detail that you think will be of help.

In most communities, you can reach police by calling 911. This number should be posted right next to the phone as, again, in threatening situations, many people panic and forget this number.

Conclusion

This chapter had a darker and more serious theme than the others in this book. I do not want you to think that bartending is a dangerous career that is full of nothing but trouble. Quite the opposite is true.

Bartending is a fabulously fun and exciting career that has been very rewarding. This chapter simply made you aware of responsibilities that you must adhere to in order to make sure that everyone in your bar has a fun and safe time. Take the topics of this chapter seriously as they are serious subjects, but do not let them keep you from seeking a career as a bartender. You will miss out on all the fun otherwise.

Review Questions

1. What is the legal age to drink in the United States?

2. What the four forms of ID should you accept as proof of age?

3. Explain backup ID. Name three examples of backup ID.

4. When should you refuse service to a guest?

5. Name three signs of intoxication.

Answers

1. The legal age to drink in the United States is 21.

2. The four forms of ID that you should accept as proof of age are a state issued driver's license, a state issued ID card, a passport or a U.S. Military ID.

3. Backup ID is an form of ID that is used to reinforce one of the four IDs that are acceptable as proof of age. This is used if the appearance of the bearer has changed since the photo was taken. Aging, shaving, and dying of the hair can change the appearance of the IDs owner dramatically. Examples of backup ID are a social security card, a bank card or a birth certificate.

4. You should refuse service to a guest when it is apparent that they are intoxicated or cannot produce satisfactory ID.

5. Three signs of intoxication are redness in the face, slurred speech and poor balance.

Chapter 9
Finding A Job

In this book we have discussed many facts and skills that you will need as a bartender. No skill, however, is more important than being able to find employment. Without this absolutely required ability, you will not be able to start you career as a bartender. This chapter is entirely dedicated to exploring this aspect of bartending.

In this chapter we are going to discuss various bartending environments. These short descriptions will discuss what you can expect if you work in one of these bars or restaurants. Beyond this, we will talk about ways to get your foot in the door without experience. This will be important and offers you a very realistic starting point for your career that will be easy to achieve. We will also discuss ways to find jobs and how to present yourself. Lastly, we will discuss what managers are looking for and how to sell yourself to a potential employer.

Bartending Environments

There are many different types of bars that you can work in. In this section we are going to briefly cover the major types of bars and discuss each style's strengths and weaknesses.

The Neighborhood Bar

Just about every neighborhood in America will have a neighborhood bar. They are just as common as a post office or convenience store. These bars tend to be smaller than large chain locations and have often been in continuous operation for decades on end if not more than a century

Neighborhood bars draw most of their customer base from the surrounding neighborhood. It is rare that people travel long distances to visit these bars. As an extension of this, these bars are heavily dependent on regular customers. If you work in one of these bars you will often see the same face over and over. This is a good thing and allows you to develop a very intimate and personal relationship with your customer base.

Neighborhood bars always run with a small staff of just a few people. It is possible that you will be the only one working on shift. If this is something that makes you uncomfortable, ask about it during the interview. Also, if the bar serves food and you are the only person working, you will need to cook as well. The need to work as a cook as well a bartender is something that you should be comfortable with, before you accept the job.

A neighborhood bar is a great place to start your bartending career. Since they are somewhat slower than large nightclubs or chain restaurants, they allow you time to refine and practice your skills. Additionally, these bars are almost always owned by individuals rather than national corporations. This permits you to make a personal appeal to the owner to give you a chance. In most cases the owner will be the one who interviews you. If not, they will almost certainly be involved in the decision to hire you.

Catering Bartending

Catering companies always need bartenders to work their catered events. This can be another great place to refine your skills and gain some experience when you are first starting out as a bartender.

A catering bartender will be required to go to the location where the catered event is happening and provide service behind the bar. This may mean that you go to a person's house, a corporate headquarters, sports arena, wedding chapel, etc.

You will almost always be required to set up and dismantle your bar using the catering company's equipment. This means that catering bartending will require you to spend time moving equipment and setting it up in addition to the time you spend serving drinks. If heavy lifting and drive time are not something that you are interested in, a catering bartending position is probably not for you. However, if you are willing to accept these tasks, working as a catering bartender can be a great experience.

Working behind the bar at a catered event is often a lot of fun as well. Catered events are almost always a happy occasion. People are getting married, retiring, getting promoted or are celebrating the holidays. This means that people are often happy and relaxed and this fills your work environment with positive energy. Also, because people often do not have to pay for their drinks (the host frequently picks up the tab) people are frequently very generous with their tips.

Casual Dining Bar

Casual dining is an industry term that describes restaurants and bars that serve meals in the $8-$18 range. These establishments are often large national restaurant companies that have outlets all over the country. Restaurants of this nature can always be found in and around malls in suburbia.

Casual dining companies will be reluctant to hire you as a bartender without any experience. This means that you may have to work to build your resume and gain experience before you can look to these companies for employment.

However, once you get your foot in the door of one of these companies, they can be a very rewarding experience. These companies spend billions each year on advertising. This means that people know and trust these companies and their brands. As a result of this effort, these companies are very busy and provide lots of thirsty customers who in turn provide lots of tips.

Additionally, these companies offer benefit packages that neighborhood bars will have trouble competing with. These benefits include insurance, stock options and 401(k). These benefits often add to the pay you receive in the form of tips and wages. In addition to these benefits, these companies frequently offer advancement in the company. If you ever grow tired of bartending you can always apply for other jobs within the company and have a good chance of getting them.

Another benefit of working for one off these companies is that it offers you the chance to move around the country, if that appeals to you. Since these companies have nationwide outlets, you can often transfer from one store to another with little difficulty. This can be a huge benefit if you decide to go back to school in California and have to move there from Minnesota.

The Pub

Small scale brewing operations have become very common across the country. These are often called "brewpubs" or "microbreweries". These bars are often owned locally like a neighborhood bar, but permit minors during part of the business day like a casual dining restaurant.

Food is always provided and these pubs are often very popular with locals who will bring in their whole family in for dinner. In many cases, pizzas make up a large part of the menu along with sandwiches, pastas and salads. The kids can enjoy nonalcoholic drinks while the parents enjoy a pint of their favorite locally produced beer. Since on-site brewing makes up a large part of these bar's business plan, you will be required to have a good beer knowledge when you work at these bars. You will need to be very familiar with beer styles and be able to accurately discuss them with guests on a frequent basis.

These bars frequently have a much more casual attitude and a dress code that is similar in style to the neighborhood bar. Employees often dress in their own clothes according to their own style, provided it adheres to the company's dress code. This casual attitude can make working a little more fun. I do not like wearing ties and these are almost never required in a pub.

These bars are another good pace to try and gain experience when you are first starting out. Again, like neighborhood bars, the owner will often be very involved in the business and can make a snap decision to hire you.

Fine Dining

Fine dining is a loose industry term that describes restaurants that have fancy, expensive entrees and provides a luxurious dining environment. These restaurants are often the restaurants that people go out to for special occasions such as birthdays and anniversaries.

Fine dining restaurants will also be reluctant to hire you as a bartender when you are first starting out. They have high standards and can afford to be discriminating in who they hire. The people that they do hire, they will hold to high and exacting standards that you will need to adhere to religiously. A guest paying $50 for a steak will expect quick and professional service no matter what drink the order.

If you do find a job in one of these restaurants it can often be a very rewarding position. Due to their high prices, guests in these restaurants often run up large bills and include equally proportioned tips as well. Also, these environments tend to be slower paced than casual dining restaurants. In a casual dining restaurant, the guest is usually in and out of the door within one hour. Conversely, in fine dining restaurants and bars, guests will expect a more leisurely service and often will spend many hours in conversation enjoying their many courses and cocktails.

Nightclubs

Nightclubs are lively dance clubs and bars that are very popular on the weekends. Wherever your town has its popular strip, you will find the nightclubs.

Usually a nightclub's business is almost exclusively derived from alcohol sales. Food is often available, but is not ordered nearly as much. Also, a nightclub's customer base is generally much younger than other bars. These are environments whose popular music and opportunities for meeting other single young people draw in the crowds. The fact that the customer base is so young means that carding is especially important in nightclubs. Nightclubs also have a higher incidence of fights and often have a dedicated security staff.

Nightclub bars are usually high production, high volume, and intense bartending environments. These are not the bars for the beginner but are an excellent place to seek a job once you have established a good amount of experience and are confident behind the bar. If you do land a job in a nightclub, the tips can be fantastic. I have known bartenders who made up to $500 a night! The high volume sales that will occur in a nightclub tend to generate mountains of money.

Small Hotel Bars

Many smaller hotels that are considered business class have small restaurants and bars that exist for the benefit of their customers. These restaurants and bars often operate in an unprofitable condition simply as a service to the guests of the hotel.

These bars are often a great place to gain experience. They are slower environments and often only have guests when the hotel is full. This means that you can focus on your skills and build them over time. Also, because of the slower environment, there is less pressure and any mistakes can quickly be fixed. To find bars of this type, try looking around the airport in your area.

Production Bartending

Many busy restaurants and bars will have a dedicated production bar. This bar is used exclusively to make drinks that are ordered by servers for delivery to tables. These bars are not accessible by guests so the bartender focuses only on "producing" drinks, hence the name. Often times, these bars are located near the kitchen area in the back of the house. This type of bar setup is common in comedy clubs and dinner theaters where the noise of a bartender interacting with guests would disturb the performers.

Production bars can be just as stressful as bars where you deal with guests as well. If a restaurant or bar is busy enough to have a dedicated production bartender on staff, they will be making a lot of drinks. However, a production bartending job can be a great place for a beginner to refine their art. Since all you are doing is making drinks and there is no worrying about serving guests, you can focus on that part of your job and get really good at it.

Another reason that makes production bartending a good place for a beginner to start is that the tips tend to be less than in a bar where you would be serving guests and servers. Instead of receiving tips from the guests, you will only be tipped by the servers. This is still a good amount of money and makes the job worth your while, but you can usually make more by interacting with guests as well. This fact makes these jobs seem less desirable to experienced bartenders, so you will not be in heavy competition with seasoned veterans. This means you stand a better chance of landing the job.

Industry Bar

People that work in the restaurant and bar industry often enjoy a cocktail or two after work. This is a fact. Actually, often times the entire crew of a restaurant will meet at a local bar after work for drinks and conversation. This type of bar is called an "industry bar". An industry bar can be a neighborhood bar or a casual dining bar. The only necessity is that the bar stays open later than any of the other restaurants or bars in the area.

Bars that are filled with cocktail waitresses, waiters, and other bartenders are often extremely profitable. The clientele understands the demands of the service industry and often tip very well. Working in an industry bar is one of the most profitable bartending jobs you can find. The one downside to working in an industry bar is that you will often work well into the late hours of the morning and you don't get to go have a drink after work.

If the bar is a neighborhood bar, again, this is a good place to try and find a job initially and gain some valuable experience.

How To Find A Bartending Job

When you were first born you needed to learn to crawl, then walk and finally run. Bartending is no different. When you are finished reading this book, we could say that you are ready to start crawling behind the bar. You are a rookie without any experience. This book has given you a good base of knowledge about bartending, now you need to augment that knowledge with experience. This means you need to find a job.

In the pages that follow, I am going to talk about how to find a bartending job. It may not be easy. I had to work early mornings for quite a while before anyone would even consider letting me behind a bar on Friday night. I had to show a lot of patience and I had to stick with it and keep my goal in sight. I did and it has paid off wonderfully. With hard work and dedication, I have faith that anyone can repeat what I have done.

Be Perseverant

It is very unlikely that you will be hired for the first job that you apply for. You are going to need to get used to a little rejection and realize that it is not the end of the world.

One tactic that I used in the past when I was actively looking for a job was by setting a simple and easy to manage goal. Usually, I would make a deal with myself that I would fill out one application per day. That meant each day I would get up, go out and find somewhere to apply for a job. I would either fill out an application (more common) or leave a resume with the manager. This was easy to do and only took a few hours each day, if that. Also, because I was only applying for one job (maybe two) per day, I did not have to spend all day being rejected. This was good for my ego and kept me from feeling totally defeated.

Most of the time, I would hear nothing back. I got used to this. You should to. Not everywhere you will want to work is going to be hiring. However, I kept at my goal each time until I landed a job.

Where To Look For A Job

There are many places to look for a bartending job. You just need to know where to look.

When I first started working as a bartender the best place to look for a job as a bartender was in the local classifieds in the newspaper.

This section was immensely helpful and could be searched using the job you wanted or what part of town you wanted to work in. Even today, newspapers are a great resource and are easy to find. Additionally, large towns and cities often have newspapers that are dedicated to nothing but employment ads. Don't overlook these when you are searching for a job.

The Internet has replaced the newspaper as the place where people go to look for a job these days. It is always on, and it is always current. New ads appear all the time. There are so many employment sites these days that I will not list them. To find an employment site that is relevant to your city, I would suggest using a search engine. Type in the search string "**Your City** employment" and see what you find. Of course, replace "Your City" with the actual name of your town.

Online classifieds are another great place to look for work. Local newspapers as well as sites such as www.craigslist.org , provide great resources you would be foolish to overlook.

If you do not feel up to searching for a job on your own, you can seek the services of an employment agency. There are two types of agencies that can help in this case.

The first type of agency that can be useful is a government agency. Your local department of labor and industries will often have offices in major cities to help citizens find work. They can assist with job counseling as well and will even help you put together a resume.

The second type of employment agency is a private firm that is working for a profit. These companies receive fees from employers when they deliver employees. There should not be a cost to you at any point and if there is, it is best to walk away. These companies often pair employers with employees for seasonal or temporary work, especially around the holidays. This is especially relevant to bartending as many catering companies hire seasonal staff to help work busy holiday and wedding seasons. Look for these companies in your local phonebook or online.

Set Your Sights Appropriately

When you are new to bartending, you need to set your sights appropriately and realize that you are going to have to pay your dues before you start working weekend nights behind the bar. You will also have little chance of landing a bartending position at your city's premier dining restaurant. Before you can hope to obtain a job in these bars, you will need to build up a little experience.

Also, when you are first starting out, don't let pride get in your way. Any experience behind the bar will help you in your quest to become the greatest bartender around. We all need to start somewhere.

Some People Lie

I am not advising you to lie on an application. Personally, I believe this to be dishonest and wrong. I did not do this when I was looking for my first bartending job and I would not suggest you do it either. Lying about your experience on an application can give you a bad reputation and be grounds for immediate dismissal. All that being said; I know people that have lied on their resumes and applications and have been hired as a result.

The Barback

Many busy bars have a position that is known as the "barback". The barback is essentially the bartender's apprentice. This person works behind the bar, but does not make drinks. Instead, they support the bartender in anyway that the bartender deems necessary, short of making drinks. Often the barback will be involved in stocking, cleaning, breaks, running food, changing kegs, etc.

While a barback position may not seem as glamorous as working as a bartender, it can be a great place to start your career. Even better is that working as a barback requires almost no experience at all. This book should provide you with the vast majority of the knowledge you need to work in this position. A little common sense should be all that you need to add.

Working as a barback is great on the job training. You will quickly learn where everything is in the bar and how the bar operates. If you study the drink recipes and pay attention, you will have everything you need to start working as a bartender if one of the bartenders quits or gets fired. Also, when this happens, the bar manager already knows and trusts you (if you have been a model employee) and will be much more willing to take a chance by making you a bartender.

If you are ever offered a barback position as a rookie bartender, snatch it up right away. Also, whenever you fill out an application and it ask you what job you are applying for, put "Bartender or Barback". This will leave the door open and let the manager know that you are willing to start at the bottom and work your way up.

Get Your Foot In The Door

If you really want to work at a particular location and they will not hire you to work as a bartender based on your level of experience, you can always ask about other positions in their organization with the aim of getting your foot in the door. Depending on your experience level in the restaurant and bar industry, you can always offer to work as a cook, server, busboy, host or dishwasher.

I know, because I did it, that you can work your way from a busboy to a bartender. It will take time and hard work. What you will need to do is to convince the owner/manager that you are worth the time and money it will take to train you to work in their bar. Show them that you are a responsible and hard working employee who cares for their guests as much as they do and you will have a good shot after some time.

You need to be willing to put in the time, however. You cannot work for a week as a dishwasher and expect to become the lead bartender. You need to understand that this will take at least six months, more likely a year. Get to know everyone in the restaurant and learn how to do as much as you can while you are waiting for your opportunity. When it comes, you will be ready.

Preparing A Resume

Depending on where you apply, you may need to present a resume. A resume is simply a sheet of paper that lists you experience, qualifications, goals and education.

Many resume templates are available for the major word processing programs. These have simple fill in the blank type inputs that make creating a professional looking resume a breeze. I would strongly recommend that you take advantage of one of these templates when you are putting a resume together.

The first and most important bits of information that should be present on a resume are your name and contact information. These should be right at the top. Restaurant managers are not going to look very hard for this information and will pass on you if the can't find it.

Example Resume: This example shows the basic form your resume should take.

John Doe
123 North Anystreet, Anytown USA 555-555-5555

Objective

My long time career goal is to find employment working as a bartender in a busy, high volume environment.

Experience

1. Anytown Bar & Grill   April 2004-Present   Anytown ,USA

    Head Bartender

I have worked at the Anytown Bar & Grill since April 2004. The position I held at this restaurant was that of Head Bartender. My duties included ordering liquor and bar supplies, scheduling and working the busiest shifts as the bartender.

2. Anytown Hotel   June 2002 – April 2004   Anytown, USA

    Bartender

I worked at the Anytown Hotel for almost two years. This hotel was dedicated to business travelers. I worked behind the bar five shifts each week and was responsible for ordering liquor, beer and wine each week.

3. Anytown Restaurant   January 1998-June 2002   Anytown, USA

    Server

I worked at the Anytown Restaurant for almost four years. I started working at this restaurant as a host and was promoted to server. I worked as a server for two years. My duties at the Anytown Restaurant included caring for guests in my section, as well as helping other servers with all aspects of table service.

Education

1. Anytown Community College   September 1998-June 2001   Anytown, USA

    Associates Degree of Science

2. Anytown High School   1994-1998   Anytown, USA

References Available upon request

Beyond listing your contact information on your resume, your experience is the most important part. This is where you list what you have done that makes you qualified for the job you are searching for.

List any experience from most recent to least recent. This will let you prospective employer see what you are doing now and what you have done in the past. Even if your past work experience is not related to bartending, include it. Add emphasis to any promotions you received. This will show that you are a hard worker and are worth taking a chance on. There is also no need to explain why you left past jobs.

After experiences, you should list any education you have received. Again, this is done from most recent to least recent. You do not need to list anything less than high school. You will just look silly if you list what elementary school you attended.

The last piece of information that is often included on resumes is any relevant references. It is common to simply write "Available upon request" in this part. Not many people will ask for these, but if they do, make sure you are ready with an answer. Try to include any past bosses or managers as references. This will be a definite plus.

Filling Out An Application

Many national bar and restaurant chains will not be interested in a resume. Instead, they will want you to fill out a standardized application form.

Most of the information that is on your resume will need to be copied over to any application that you fill out. As such, I always take a resume or two with me when I go to fill out applications. On your resume, all of the needed information is organized and can easily be copied to the application.

If there are any questions on the application whose answers are not on the resume, answer them to the best of your abilities in an honest fashion. Finally, sign the application where it asks you to.

Preparing For An Interview

If your resume or application does its work, you will be offered an interview. You need to show up to any interview prepared and looking professional.

The first area of business is your dress code. When preparing for an interview you need to think about the bar where you will be interviewing. What is their manner of dress? My advice in selecting your wardrobe is to dress semi-casual. Do not dress too fancy, such as wearing a tux or evening gown. Make sure you are presentable and dressed conservatively. Do not let exposed chest hair or excessive cleavage cost you a job. You can always relax and let your hair down a little once you have the job, but until then error on the side of caution.

There are also several documents and pieces of ID that you should always take with you to a job interview. You never know and they may hire you on the spot. The faster you can provide all the necessary paperwork, the faster you can start working and making money.

If your state requires you to have an alcohol service permit, make sure you take this with you. If you do not have one, you should have a date set as to when you will get one. This will show you are versed in the requirements of your job and are organized enough to take care of business.

A food handler's permit is also required by many counties. These permits are given to people once they have passed a basic food safety course. This course is easy and the test is basically repetition. Many counties offer their courses online. This is the best and easiest way to get one of these permits. You can pay online with a credit card and print out your card instantly. You should have one of these, if required, before you go to the interview.

Additionally, you will need to take enough ID to fill out a Department of Justice Form I-9. This form states that you are a United States citizen or are otherwise permitted to work in the U.S. All you need to take is your driver's license or ID card along with either a passport or your Social Security card. Showing up without these is a bad idea because it tells your employer that you are not organized or prepared.

The other two things that you should always take with you to an interview are a copy of your resume and a pen. The resume will be right there if you need to refer to it during the interview. The person interviewing you may not bring your resume or application with them. The pen will be handy if you need to fill out any paperwork and again, shows that you are prepared, organized and serious.

The Interview – What a manager looks for

When a manager interviews you they are really looking you over and getting to know you before they decide to hire you. Often, they will be inclined to hire you simply based on what your application or resume says and are using the interview as a means to size you up.

The person that will always get hired is the person who will make the manager's job easier and accomplish their tasks in an organized, responsible, and professional manner. During the interview process, you want to convince your interviewer that you are this person.

One way to show the manager that you are a person that will make their job easier is to stress that you are willing to work whenever you are needed. Every bar or restaurant has shifts that no one wants to work. These shifts are during the slower parts of the week or are early in the morning. As a rule, bar people tend to like to work at night. As a result of this, many managers have to wrestle with filling these shifts. If you are a person who tells them that you would be happy to pick up these undesirable shifts, you will often win points in their book.

Stressing your professionalism during your interview cannot be emphasized enough. If the manager chooses to hire you, they are entrusting you with their bar's guests. It can honestly be stated that the guests are the most valuable asset a bar has. Money stolen out of the cash register pales in comparison to alienating the guests and making them not return.

To help put across that you are a professional worker who takes their job seriously, avoid using profanity during the interview and conduct yourself in a respectable manner. Also, point out any experiences from your resume, such as a promotion, that show you have been dedicated to your work.

Your interviewer will ask you a series of questions during the interview process. These questions are often standard interview questions that are approved by the company's Human Resources Department. You need to answer these questions honestly and quickly. Answer the questions honestly even if you do not like the answer. An example of this would be why you were fired from a job in the past. Explain what happened in a forthright manner.

Don't try to overthink the questions either. Answer them with the first answer that comes to mind. Most of the time your first instinct will be the right one.

The last thing that I want you remember about an interview is to remain calm. This can be hard at times. Many people get very nervous during an interview. If you feel that you are getting a little excited, stop and take a deep breath. You are going to be OK.

Conclusion

This chapter discussed many points that you will need to keep in mind when you are looking for a job as a bartender. However, this is really up to you. You are the one that needs to go out and pound the pavement and find a place for yourself in the local bartending community. Work hard and stay determined and you will find a place to start.

Once you have found a spot, work hard and be willing to help wherever you can and there is not telling how far you can go!

Homework Assignment #3 – Prepare A Resume

This chapter was all about finding a job as a bartender. As such, the homework assignment for this chapter is simply to prepare a resume that you can use when looking for a job as a bartender.

To prepare a resume, you may use the example resume that was included in this chapter. If you do not like the style of that resume, consult your local library. There are many, many books out there that discuss assembling a resume in depth. These are a great resource if you are uncertain where to begin.

Afterword

Hopefully, you the reader have found this book to be informative and helpful. Many times, before starting out with something new, say a career, the hardest part is knowing where to start. It is my sincere hope that you now know where to start and have many of the tools to make yourself successful.

Like I said in the beginning, this book is not a guarantee of success. You will need to add your hard work, dedication and perseverance to what you learned from reading this book. You will also need to continue learning and refining your skills. If you stick with it and work hard, there is no reason you cannot be successful. Good luck!

-Thomas Morrell

Appendix
Basic Drink Recipes

Gin & Tonic, Soda, 7

Basic Form: Liquor & Mixer

Glass: Bucket or Collins

1. Fill glass with ice.
2. Add one shot of gin.
3. Fill glass with tonic, soda, or lemon & lime soda.
4. Garnish with a lime.

Whiskey & Cola, Soda, 7

Basic Form: Liquor & Mixer

Glass: Bucket or Collins

1. Fill glass with ice.
2. Add one shot of whiskey.
3. Fill glass with cola, soda or lemon & lime soda.
4. No garnish

Vodka & Energy Drink

Basic Form: Liquor & Mixer

Glass: Bucket or Collins

1. Fill glass with ice.
2. Add one shot of vodka.
3. Fill glass with an energy drink of your choosing
4. Garnish with a lime and cherry

Hairy Navel

Basic Form: Double Liquor & Mixer

Glass: Bucket or Collins

1. Fill glass with ice.
2. Add one shot of peach schnapps and one shot of vodka.
3. Fill glass with orange juice.
4. Garnish with an orange and a cherry.

Vodka & Tonic, Soda, 7

Basic Form: Liquor & Mixer

Glass: Bucket or Collins

1. Fill glass with ice.
2. Add one shot of vodka.
3. Fill glass with tonic, soda, or lemon & lime soda.
4. Garnish with a lime.

Rum & Cola or Diet Cola

Basic Form: Liquor & Mixer

Glass: Bucket or Collins

1. Fill glass with ice.
2. Add one shot of rum.
3. Fill glass with cola or diet
4. No garnish.

Vodka & Cranberry/Cape Cod

Basic Form: Liquor & Mixer

Glass: Bucket or Collins

1. Fill glass with ice.
2. Add one shot of vodka.
3. Fill glass with cranberry juice.
4. Garnish with a lime.

Greyhound

Basic Form: Liquor & Mixer

Glass: Bucket or Collins

1. Fill glass with ice.
2. Add one shot of vodka.
3. Fill glass with grapefruit juice.
4. Garnish with a grapefruit slice.

Salty Dog

Basic Form: Liquor & Mixer

Glass: Bucket or Collins

1. Rim the glass with salt.
2. Fill glass with ice.
3. Add one shot of vodka
4. Fill with grapefruit juice.
5. Garnish with a grapefruit slice.

Margarita

Basic Form: Double Liquor & Mixer

Glass: Bucket, Collins, Pint Glass or Martini Glass

1. Salt the rim of whatever glass you are using. If using pint, bucket, or Collins glass fill with ice. No ice for cocktail glass.
2. Fill shaker with ice.
3. Add one shot of tequila, one half shot of triple sec, two ounces of lime and two sugar cubes **or** one shot of simple syrup.
4. Shake.
5. Strain mix into glass.
6. Garnish with a lime.

Fruit Daiquiri

Glass: Daiquiri Glass

1. Fill glass with ice.
2. Pour ice into blender. Add one half scoop of ice into blender.
3. Add one shot of rum, lime juice and simple syrup.
4. Add 2-4 ounces of fruit to blender. You can use strawberry, raspberry, peach, banana or even melon.
5. Sugar rim the glass.
6. Blend.
7. Pour mixture into glass.
8. Garnish with a lime and fruit.

Screwhound

Basic Form: Liquor & Mixer

Glass: Bucket or Collins

1. Fill glass with ice.
2. Add one shot of vodka.
3. Fill glass with half orange and grapefruit juice.
4. Garnish with orange and grapefruit.

Cadillac Margarita

Basic Form: Double Liquor & Mixer

Glass: Bucket, Collins, Pint Glass

1. Salt the rim of whatever glass you are using. If using pint, bucket, or Collins glass fill with ice.
2. Fill shaker with ice.
3. Add one shot of tequila, one half shot of triple sec, two ounces of lime and two sugar cubes **or** one shot of simple syrup.
4. Shake.
5. Strain mix into glass.
6. Float with top shelf orange brandy.
6. Garnish with a lime.

Pina Colada

Glass: Daiquiri Glass

1. Fill glass with ice.
2. Pour ice into blender and add one half scoop more.
3. Add one shot of rum, cream, coconut extract, and pineapple juice.
4. Blend.
5. Pour mixture into glass.
6. Garnish glass with pineapple and a cherry joined with a toothpick.

Coconut Rum & Pineapple

Basic Form: Liquor & Mixer

Glass: Bucket or Collins

1. Fill glass with ice.
2. Add one shot of coconut rum.
3. Fill glass with pineapple juice.
4. Garnish with a pineapple slice.

Sea Breeze

Basic Form: Liquor & Mixer

Glass: Bucket or Collins

1. Fill glass with ice.
2. Add one shot of vodka.
3. Fill glass with half grapefruit juice and half cranberry.
4. Garnish with a lime and cherry.

White Russian

Basic Form: Double Liquor & Mixer

Glass: Bucket or Collins

1. Fill glass with ice.
2. Add one shot of vodka and one half shot of coffee liquor.
3. Fill glass with cream.
4. No garnish.

Mind Eraser

Basic Form: Double Liquor & Mixer

Glass: Bucket or Collins

1. Fill glass with ice.
2. Add one shot of vodka and one half shot of coffee liquor.
3. Fill glass with soda.
4. No garnish.

Bloody Mary

Basic Form: Liquor & Mixer

Glass: Pint Glass

1. Rim glass with salt.
2. Fill glass with ice.
3. Add one shot of vodka.
4. Fill glass with Bloody Mary mix.
5. Garnish with celery, olives, garlic, asparagus or lime.

Bloody Maria

Basic Form: Liquor & Mixer

Glass: Pint Glass

1. Rim glass with salt.
2. Fill glass with ice.
3. Add one shot of tequila.
4. Fill glass with Bloody Mary mix.
5. Garnish with celery, olives, garlic, asparagus or lime.

Black Russian

Glass: Bucket

1. Fill glass with ice.
2. Add one shot of vodka and one half shot of coffee liquor.
3. No garnish.

Coffee Liquor & Cream

Basic Form: Liquor & Mixer

Glass: Bucket or Collins

1. Fill glass with ice.
2. Add one shot of coffee liquor.
3. Fill glass with cream.
4. No garnish.

Smith & Wesson

Basic Form: Liquor & Mixer

Glass: Bucket or Collins

1. Fill glass with ice.
2. Add one shot of coffee liquor.
3. Fill glass with half cream and half cola.
4. No garnish.

Brandy Separator

Basic Form: Double Liquor & Mixer

Glass: Bucket or Collins

1. Fill glass with ice.
2. Add one shot of brandy and one half shot of coffee liquor.
3. Fill glass with cream.
4. No garnish.

Colorado Bulldog

Basic Form: Double Liquor & Mixer

Glass: Collins or Daiquiri Glass

1. Fill glass with ice.
2. Add one shot of vodka and one shot of coffee liquor.
3. Fill glass with half cream and half cola.
4. Garnish glass with a cherry.

Whiskey & Sour Mix

Basic Form: Liquor & Mixer

Glass: Bucket or Collins

1. Fill glass with ice.
2. Add one shot of whiskey.
3. Fill glass with sour mix.
4. Garnish with a lime and a cherry.

Smith & Kerns

Basic Form: Liquor & Mixer

Glass: Bucket or Collins

1. Fill glass with ice.
2. Add one shot of coffee liquor.
3. Fill glass with half cream and half soda.
4. No garnish.

Panty Dropper

Basic Form: Double Liquor & Mixer

Glass: Bucket or Collins

1. Fill glass with ice.
2. Add one shot vodka and one half shot sloe gin.
3. Fill with cream.
4. Garnish with a cherry.

Amaretto & Sour Mix

Basic Form: Liquor & Mixer

Glass: Bucket or Collins

1. Fill glass with ice.
2. Add one shot of amaretto liquor.
3. Fill glass with sour mix.
4. Garnish with a lime and cherry.

Amaretto & Sour Mix

Basic Form: Liquor & Mixer

Glass: Bucket or Collins

1. Fill glass with ice.
2. Add one shot of amaretto liquor.
3. Fill glass with sour mix.
4. Garnish with a lime and cherry.

Tequila Sunrise

Basic Form: Liquor & Mixer

Glass: Bucket or Collins

1. Fill glass with ice.

2. Add one shot of tequila.

3. Fill glass with orange juice.

4. Add a dash of grenadine to give a red color to the drink.

5. Garnish with an orange.

Alabama Slammer

Glass: Bucket or Collins

1. Fill glass with ice.

2. Add one shot Southern Comfort™, one half shot of amaretto and one half shot sloe gin.

3. Fill with orange juice.

4. Garnish with an orange and a cherry.

Slow Comfortable Screw

Basic Form: Double Liquor & Mixer

Glass: Bucket or Collins

1. Fill glass with ice.

2. Add one shot of sloe gin and one half shot Southern Comfort™.

3. Fill glass with orange juice.

4. Garnish with an orange and a cherry.

Tom Collins

Basic Form: Liquor & Mixer

Glass: Collins

1. Fill glass with ice.

2. Add one shot of gin, 2 ounces of lemon or lime juice, one shot of simple syrup and shake.

3. Return mix to glass and fill with lemon & lime soda.

4. Garnish with a lime and a cherry.

Sex On The Beach

Basic Form: Double Liquor & Mixer

Glass: Bucket or Collins

1. Fill glass with ice.

2. Add one shot of vodka and one half shot of peach schnapps.

3. Fill glass with half orange and half cranberry.

4. Garnish with an orange and a cherry.

Harvey Wallbanger

Basic Form: Liquor & Mixer

Glass: Bucket or Collins

1. Fill glass with ice.

2. Add one shot of vodka.

3. Fill with orange juice.

4. Pour a float of Galliano™ liquor.

5. Garnish with an orange and a cherry.

Slow Comfortable Screw Against A Wall

Basic Form: Double Liquor & Mixer

Glass: Bucket or Collins

1. Fill glass with ice.

2. Add one shot of sloe gin and one half shot of Southern Comfort™.

3. Fill glass with orange juice.

4. Add a float of Galliano™.

5. Garnish with orange and a cherry.

John Collins

Basic Form: Liquor & Mixer

Glass: Collins

1. Fill glass with ice.

2. Add one shot of whiskey, 2 ounces of lemon or lime juice, one shot of simple syrup and shake.

3. Return mix to glass and fill with lemon & lime soda.

4. Garnish with a lime and a cherry.

Vodka Collins

Basic Form: Liquor & Mixer

Glass: Collins

1. Fill glass with ice.

2. Add one shot of vodka, 2 ounces of lemon or lime juice, one shot of simple syrup and shake.

3. Return mix to glass and fill with lemon & lime soda.

4. Garnish with a lime and a cherry.

Old Fashioned

Basic Form: Liquor & Mixer

Glass: Bucket

1. Place orange slice and a cherry in the glass. Fill glass with ice.

2. Muddle mix until fruit is crushed.

3. Add one shot of whiskey to the glass.

4. Fill glass with soda water.

Rusty Nail

Basic Form: Double Liquor & Mixer

Glass: Rocks or Bucket

1. Fill glass with ice.

2. Add one shot of scotch and one half shot of Dramboie™

3. No garnish.

Dirty Mother

Basic Form: Double Liquor & Mixer

Glass: Bucker or Collins

1. Fill glass with ice.

2. Add one shot of brandy and one half shot of coffee liquor.

3. Fill glass with half & half.

4. Garnish with a cherry.

Cuba Librė

Basic Form: Liquor & Mixer

Glass: Bucket

1. Fill glass with ice.

2. Add one shot of rum.

3. Fill glass with cola.

4. Garnish with a lime.

Surfer on Acid

Basic Form: Double Liquor & Mixer

Glass: Bucket

1. Fill glass with ice.

2. Add one shot of Jagermeister™ and one half shot of coconut rum.

3. Fill glass with pineapple juice.

4. Garnish with a pineapple.

This drink can also be served as a chilled shot with less pineapple.

Snakebite

Basic Form: Liquor & mIxer

Glass: Rocks or Bucket

1. Fill glass with ice.

2. Add one shot of Yukon Jack™ Canadian Whiskey.

3. Add one half shot of lime juice.

4. No garnish.

Root Beer Float

Basic Form: Double Liquor & Mixer

Glass: Collins or Pint

1. Fill glass with ice.

2. Add one shot of Galliano™ and one half shot of vodka.

3. Fill glass with equal parts cola and half & half.

4. Garnish with a cherry.

Dead Nazi

Glass: Shot or Rocks

1. Shake over ice one shot of Jagermeister™ and one half shot of peppermint schnapps.

2. Strain into glass.

Buttery Nipple

Glass: Rocks or Shot

1. Mix in glass, one shot of Irish cream and one half shot of butterscotch schnapps.

Slippery Nipple

Glass: Rocks or Shot

1. Mix in glass, one half shot of Irish Cream, one half shot of butterscotch schnapps and one half shot of coffee liquor.

Variations of this drink exist that use licorice liquor in place of the butterscotch. Most people ordering this drink do not have that in mind.

B-52

Glass: Rocks or Shot

1. Layer in the glass (in order) one half shot coffee liquor, one half Irish cream and one half shot of amaretto. Use a cherry or spoon.

Three Wise Man

Glass: Shot or Rocks

1. Add to glass one half shot of Jack Daniel's™, one half shot Jim Beam™, and one half shot Johnny Walker™.

Brain Hemorrhage

Glass: Shot or Rocks

1. Pour one shot of peach schnapps into glass.

2. Pouring over a spoon or cherry, add one half shot of Irish cream into the center of the glass. It will float on the schnapps and create a blob.

3. Into blob, add a dash of grenadine.

German Chocolate Cake

Glass: Rocks or Shot

1. In glass mix one shot of citrus vodka and one half shot Frangelico™ Hazelnut liquor.

2. Garnish with a sugared lemon.

To take the shot, drink and then bite the lemon. This gives the exact flavor of chocolate cake.

Duck Fart

Glass: Rocks or Shot

1. Add to glass one half shot of Canadian whiskey, one half shot of Irish cream and one half shot of coffee liquor.

Can also be layered.

Oatmeal Cookie

Glass: Shot or Rocks

1. Mix in glass one half shot of Irish cream, one half shot of butterscotch schnapps, and one half shot cinnamon schnapps.

Cement Mixer

Glass: Rocks or Shot

1. Mix one shot of Irish cream and one half shot of lime juice.

To take this shot, drink and mix in your mouth. The cream and liquor will congeal and create a pasty substance. Hence the name.

Blowjob

Glass: Shot or Rocks

1. Mix one shot of Irish cream and one half shot of amaretto in the glass.

2. Top with a generous amount of whipped cream.

Prairie Fire

Glass: Shot or Rocks

1. Add one shot of tequila.

2. Float a good amount of hot sauce on top of the tequila.

Long Island Iced Tea

Basic Form: Long Island

Glass: Pint

1. Fill glass with ice.

2. Add one half shot of gin.

3. Add one half shot of vodka.

4. Add one half shot of rum.

5. Add one half shot of triple sec.

6. Add two ounces of sweet and sour mix or one shot of lemon juice and one half shot of simple syrup.

7. Fill with cola.

8. Garnish with a lime and a cherry.

Irish Car Bomb

Glass: Pint **AND** Shot

1. Pour one half shot of Irish whiskey and one half shot of Irish cream into the shot glass.

2. **Gently** drop shot glass into a pint glass two thirds full of stout.

3. Drink mix before it curdles.

Red Headed Slut

Glass: Rocks or Shot

1. Add one shot of Jagermeister™ and one half shot peach schnapps.

2. Fill glass with cranberry juice.

Afterburner

Glass: Shot or Rocks

1. Add one shot of cinnamon schnapps and one half shot of rum.

Tokyo Iced Tea

Basic Form: Long Island

Glass: Pint

1. Fill glass with ice.

2. Add one half shot of gin.

3. Add one half shot of vodka.

4. Add one half shot of rum.

5. Add one half shot of Midori™ Melon Liquor.

6. Add two ounces of sweet and sour mix or one shot of lemon juice and one half shot of simple syrup.

7. Fill with lemon & lime soda.

8. Garnish with a lemon and a cherry.

Texas Iced Tea
Basic Form: Long Island

Glass: Pint

1. Fill glass with ice.
2. Add one half shot of gin.
3. Add one half shot of vodka.
4. Add one half shot of rum.
5. Add one half shot of tequila.
6. Add two ounces of sweet and sour mix or one shot of lemon juice and one half shot of simple syrup.
7. Fill with cola.
8. Garnish with a lime and a cherry.

Hawaiian Iced Tea
Basic Form: Long Island

Glass: Pint

1. Fill glass with ice.
2. Add one half shot of gin.
3. Add one half shot of vodka.
4. Add one half shot of rum.
5. Add one half shot of Blue Curacao.
6. Add two ounces of pineapple juice.
7. Fill with lemon & lime soda.
8. Garnish with a pineapple and a cherry.

Miami Iced Tea
Basic Form: Long Island

Glass: Pint

1. Fill glass with ice.
2. Add one half shot of gin.
3. Add one half shot of vodka.
4. Add one half shot of rum.
5. Add one half shot of peach schnapps.
6. Add two ounces of orange juice.
7. Fill with cola.
8. Garnish with an orange and a cherry.

Darth Vader
Basic Form: Long Island

Glass: Pint

1. Fill glass with ice.
2. Add one half shot of gin.
3. Add one half shot of vodka.
4. Add one half shot of rum.
5. Add one half shot of Jagermeister™.
6. Add two ounces of sweet and sour mix or one shot of lemon juice and one half shot of simple syrup.
7. Fill with cola.
8. Garnish with a lime and a cherry.

Adios Mother Fucker (AMF)

Basic Form: Long Island

Glass: Pint

1. Fill glass with ice.
2. Add one half shot of gin.
3. Add one half shot of vodka.
4. Add one half shot of rum.
5. Add one half shot of Blue Curacao.
6. Add two ounces of sweet and sour mix or one shot of lemon juice and one half shot of simple syrup.
7. Fill with lemon & lime soda.
8. Garnish with a lime and a cherry.

Mai Tai

Glass: Pint

1. Fill glass with ice.
2. Add one half shot of light rum.
3. Add one half shot of gold rum.
4. Add one half shot of dark rum.
5. Fill glass with a mix of pineapple and orange juice.
6. Float a dash of 151 rum on the top of the drink.
7. Garnish with a pineapple, orange and cherry.

Black Pearl

Basic Form: Long Island

Glass: Pint

1. Fill glass with ice.
2. Add one half shot of gin.
3. Add one half shot of vodka.
4. Add one half shot of rum.
5. Add one half shot of raspberry liquor.
6. Add two ounces of sweet and sour mix or one shot of lemon juice and one half shot of simple syrup.
7. Fill with lemon & lime soda.
8. Garnish with a lime and a cherry.

Long Beach Iced Tea

Basic Form: Long Island

Glass: Pint

1. Fill glass with ice.
2. Add one half shot of gin.
3. Add one half shot of vodka.
4. Add one half shot of rum.
5. Add one half shot of triple sec.
6. Add two ounces of sweet and sour mix or one shot of lemon juice and one half shot of simple syrup.
7. Fill with cranberry juice.
8. Garnish with a lime and a cherry.

Kamikaze

Basic Form: Fancy Martini

Glass: Cocktail

1. Fill mixing tin with ice.
2. Add one shot of vodka.
3. Add one half shot of triple sec.
4. Add one shot of simple syrup.
5. Add about 2 ounces of lime juice.
6. Shake cocktail thoroughly.
7. Strain into a cocktail glass.
8. Garnish with a lime.

Lynchburg Lemonade

Basic From: Double Liquor & Mixer

Glass: Collins or Pint

1. Fill glass with ice.
2. Add one shot of Jack Daniel's Tennessee Whiskey™.
3. Add one half shot of triple sec.
4. Add one shot of lemon juice and one half shot of simple syrup.
5. Fill glass with lemon & lime soda.
6. Garnish with a lemon and a cherry

Cosmopolitan

Basic Form: Fancy Martini

Glass: Cocktail

1. Fill mixing tin with ice.
2. Add one shot of vodka.
3. Add one half shot of triple sec.
4. Add one shot of simple syrup.
5. Add about 2 ounces of lime juice.
6. Add a good splash of cranberry juice.
6. Shake cocktail thoroughly.
7. Strain into a cocktail glass.
8. Garnish with a lime.

Raspberry Kamikaze

Basic Form: Fancy Martini

Glass: Cocktail

1. Fill mixing tin with ice.
2. Add one shot of vodka.
3. Add one half shot of raspberry liquor.
4. Add one shot of simple syrup.
5. Add about 2 ounces of lime juice.
6. Shake cocktail thoroughly.
7. Strain into a cocktail glass.
8. Garnish with a lime.

Hurricane

Glass: Pint or Daiquiri

1. Fill glass with ice.
2. Add one shot of light rum.
3. Add one shot of dark rum.
4. Add one shot of lime juice.
5. Add one shot of passion fruit juice.
6. Fill with orange juice.
7. Garnish with an orange and a cherry.

Lemondrop

Basic Form: Fancy Martini

Glass: Cocktail

1. Fill mixing tin with ice.
2. Add one shot of vodka.
3. Add one half shot of triple sec.
4. Add one shot of simple syrup.
5. Add about 2 ounces of lemon juice.
6. Shake cocktail thoroughly.
7. Sugar rim a cocktail glass.
7. Strain into the cocktail glass.
8. Garnish with a lemon.

Orangedrop

Basic Form: Fancy Martini

Glass: Cocktail

1. Fill mixing tin with ice.
2. Add one shot of vodka.
3. Add one half shot of triple sec.
4. Add one half of simple syrup.
5. Add about 2 ounces of orange juice.
6. Shake cocktail thoroughly.
7. Sugar rim a cocktail glass.
7. Strain into the cocktail glass.
8. Garnish with a orange.

Tuaca™ Sidecar

Basic Form: Fancy Martini

Glass: Cocktail

1. Fill mixing tin with ice.
2. Add one shot of brandy.
3. Add one half shot of triple sec.
4. Add one half shot of Tuaca™ liquor.
5. Add one shot of simple syrup.
6. Add about 1 ounce of lemon juice.
7. Add about 1 ounce of orange juice
8. Shake cocktail thoroughly.
9. Strain into the cocktail glass.
10. Garnish with a orange.

Sidecar

Basic Form: Fancy Martini

Glass: Cocktail

1. Fill mixing tin with ice.
2. Add one shot of brandy.
3. Add one half shot of triple sec.
4. Add one shot of simple syrup.
5. Add about 1 ounce of lemon juice.
5. Add about 1 ounce of orange juice
6. Shake cocktail thoroughly.
7. Strain into the cocktail glass.
8. Garnish with a orange.

Washington Apple

Basic Form: Fancy Martini

Glass: Cocktail

1. Fill mixing tin with ice.
2. Add one shot of Canadian whiskey.
3. Add one half shot of sour apple liquor.
4. Add one shot of simple syrup.
5. Add about 2 ounces of cranberry juice.
5. Add a splash of lemon & lime soda.
6. Shake cocktail thoroughly.
7. Strain into the cocktail glass.
8. Garnish with a lime.

Gimlet

Basic Form: Fancy Martini

Glass: Cocktail

1. Fill mixing tin with ice.
2. Add two shots of gin or vodka.
3. Add 1 ounce of sweetened lime juice.
4. Shake thoroughly.
5. Strain into glass.
6. Garnish with a lime.

Classic Manhattan

Basic Form : Basic Martini

Glass: Cocktail

1. Fill mixing tin with ice.
2. Add two shots of bourbon.
3. Add a splash of sweet vermouth.
4. Shake thoroughly.
5. Strain into glass.
6. Garnish with one cherry.

Gibson

Basic Form : Basic Martini

Glass: Cocktail

1. Fill mixing tin with ice.
2. Add two shots of gin or vodka.
3. Add a splash of dry vermouth.
4. Shake thoroughly.
5. Strain into glass.
6. Garnish with three pearl onions.

Dirty Martini

Basic Form: Basic Martini

Glass: Cocktail

1. Fill mixing tin with ice.
2. Add two shots of gin or vodka.
3. Add a splash of dry vermouth.
4. Add 1 shot of olive juice.
4. Shake thoroughly.
5. Strain into glass.
6. Garnish with three olives.

Rob Roy

Basic Form : Basic Martini

Glass: Cocktail

1. Fill mixing tin with ice.
2. Add two shots of scotch.
3. Add a splash of sweet vermouth.
4. Shake thoroughly.
5. Strain into glass.
6. Garnish with one cherry.

Classic Martini

Basic Form : Basic Martini

Glass: Cocktail

1. Fill mixing tin with ice.
2. Add two shots of gin or vodka.
3. Add a splash of dry vermouth.
4. Shake thoroughly.
5. Strain into glass.
6. Garnish with three olives.

Apple Martini

Basic Form: Fancy Martini

Glass: Cocktail

1. Fill mixing tin with ice.

2. Add one and a half shots of apple vodka.

3. Add a half shot of sour apple liquor

4. Shake thoroughly.

5. Strain into glass.

6. Garnish with a cherry.

Chocolate Martini

Basic Form: Fancy Martini

Glass: Cocktail

1. Fill mixing tin with ice.

2. Add one and a half shots of vanilla vodka.

3. Add one half shot of light cream de cocoa

4. Shake thoroughly.

5. Strain into glass.

6. Garnish with a cherry

Irish Coffee

Glass: Coffee

1. Add two sugar cubes to glass.

2. Add a shot of hot coffee to melt cube and mix.

3. Add one shot of Irish whiskey.

4. Fill with coffee.

5. Float a layer of heavy whipping cream.

Espresso Martini

Basic Form: Fancy Martini

Glass: Cocktail

1. Fill mixing tin with ice.

2. Add two shots of vanilla vodka.

3. Add two ounces of cold espresso.

4. Shake thoroughly.

5. Strain into glass.

6. Float a layer of heavy whipping cream on top.

Scooby Snack

Glass: Cocktail

1. Fill mixing tin with ice.

2. Mix one half shot of coconut rum and one half shot of melon liquor.

3. Add one ounce of pineapple juice and one ounce of half & half

4. Shake thoroughly.

5. Strain into glass.

6. Float a layer of heavy whipping cream on top.

BFK

Glass: Coffee

1. Add one half shot of Irish cream, one half shot of coffee liquor, and one half shot of hazelnut liquor.

2. Fill with coffee.

3. Float a layer of heavy whipping cream.

Coffee Nudge

Glass: Coffee

1. Add one half shot of coffee liquor, one half shot of brandy and one half shot of dark cream de cocoa.

2. Fill with coffee.

3. Float a layer of heavy whipping cream.

Hot Toddy

Glass: Coffee

1. Add one shot of whiskey.

2. Add juice of half a lemon.

3. Add a squirt of honey.

4. Fill glass with hot water and stir.

5. Garnish with a cinnamon stick.

Blueberry Tea

Glass: Snifter

1. Add one half shot of amaretto.

2. Add one half shot Grand Marnier™.

3. Place an orange spiced tea bag in the glass.

4. Fill the glass with hot water.

Irish Monk

Glass: Coffee

1. Add one shot of Irish cream.

2. Add one half shot of hazelnut liquor.

3. Fill glass with coffee.

4. Float a layer of heavy whipping cream.

B-52 Coffee

Glass: Coffee

1. Add one half shot of Irish cream, one half shot of coffee liquor and one half shot of orange brandy.

2. Fill with coffee.

3. Float a layer of heavy whipping cream.

Peppermint Patty

Glass: Coffee

1. Add one shot of peppermint schnapps.

2. Fill glass with hot chocolate.

3. Top with whip cream.

Spanish Coffee

Glass: Coffee

1. Sugar rim the coffee glass.

2. Add one half shot of 151 run to the glass. Carefully light this on fire.

3. With your hands, carefully rotate the glass, exposing the sugared rim to the flame to caramelize the sugar. The sugar is done when it turns slightly brown.

4. Add a dash of nutmeg and cinnamon to the flame. This will flare. Customers love this part.

5. Add one half shot of coffee liquor and one half shot of triple sec.

6. Fill with coffee.

7. Float a layer of whipping cream on the coffee.

8. Garnish with a dash of nutmeg on top.

Mexican Coffee

Glass: Coffee

1. Add one shot of coffee liquor.

2. Add one half shot of tequila.

3. Fill glass with coffee.

4. Float a layer of heavy whipping cream on the coffee.

5. Garnish with a dash of cinnamon or a cinnamon stick.

Jamaican Coffee

Glass: Coffee

1. Add one shot of coffee liquor.

2. Add one half shot of white rum.

3. Fill glass with coffee.

4. Float a layer of heavy whipping cream on the coffee.

197

35549840R00118

Made in the USA
Middletown, DE
07 February 2019